nothing fancy

nothing fancy

unfussy food for having people over

ALISON ROMAN

photographs by Michael Graydon and Nikole Herriott

CLARKSON POTTER/PUBLISHERS
New York

For Grandma Prue,
who taught me about the
importance of crudité,
white wine on ice, and
a great orange-red nail

Published in the United States by
Clarkson Potter/Publishers, an imprint
of Random House, a division of Penguin
Random House LLC, New York.
clarksonpotter.com

CLARKSON POTTER is a trademark and
POTTER with colophon is a registered
trademark of Penguin Random House LLC.

Library of Congress Cataloging-in-
Publication Data is available at https://
lccn.loc.gov/2019001089.

ISBN 978-0-451-49701-7
Ebook ISBN 978-0-451-49702-4

Printed in China

Book and cover design by
Elizabeth Spiridakis Olson
Cover photographs by
Michael Graydon
and Nikole Herriott

10 9 8 7 6

First Edition

contents

snack time

salads

sides

mains

after dinner

This is not a book about entertaining.

"Roasting a nice chicken for people is such a good way to say, 'I love you.'"
I recently found this note to myself scrawled on the back of an electrical bill I had probably forgotten to pay, written one night after a dinner party. There was likely a lot of wine that night (the best ideas always come from a lot of wine), which explains my poor penmanship and well-intentioned (but fragmented) deep chicken thought.

Not exactly poetry, but I realized after reading it that it was the first time I articulated exactly what I wanted this book to be about it and what I want you to get out of it: Using your time and resources to feed people you care about is the ultimate expression of love. And love is about expressing joy, not producing anxiety, so the other thing I want you to get out of it is: You can do this.

I have always been allergic to the word "entertaining," which to me implies there's a show, something performative at best and inauthentic at worst. But having people over? Well, that's just making dinner, but you know, with more people. Unfussy food, unfussy vibes and the permission to be imperfect, no occasion necessary (other than to eat, of course).

For anyone looking for tips on how to fold linen napkins or create floral arrangements, I am not your girl. I don't have any clever hosting tips, and I will not teach you the secrets to mood lighting. (I told you, this is not an entertaining book, but also: candles!) But I will give you low-stress and high-impact recipes and ideas designed to make your life easier when cooking for others. Colorful platters of vegetables doused in crispy crunchy bits, casually roasted meat scattered with herbs, one-bowl just-sweet-enough desserts.

This book is organized by how I like to put together most meals, broken up by what I think are the five most important parts: snacks, salads, sides, mains, and sweet things. Not to say all categories must be represented to have a complete experience, but using that framework is a good place to start.

Most of the recipes serve 4 to 6 people and are designed to be doubled easily. If you're cooking for fewer than four, well then consider the bounty a gift to your future self in the form of leftovers. There are carefully considered do-aheads (my favorite phrase) and ideas for what goes with what, although I will say most things in this book would be so happy served next to one another (I find the concept of menus to be both inspiring and creatively stifling, so consider this my compromise). It's a book with a true choose-your-own-adventure spirit, encouraging you to make as many or as few of the dishes as you wish.

This is not about living an aspirational life; it's about living an attainable one. You know, the one that comes with not really having enough time to braise a whole pot of short ribs before people arrive (but you try anyway), accidentally burnt cakes (just cut those parts off), and not enough chairs to seat everyone at once (sit on the floor?). It's the life we live, it's messy as hell, it's nothing fancy—I'm sure you wouldn't want it any other way.

three helpful things

1
ask for help

"Asking for help is not a weakness, it's a strength."
—me to myself every time I cook for others

If you're a control freak like me, delegating does not come easily. But come to think of your guests as contributors and collaborators and you'll notice everyone loosen up, things happen more quickly, and the whole vibe gets significantly more fun. Asking guests to participate by picking the stems from herbs, mixing a yogurt sauce, or slicing vegetables is a small but significant way to ease the load.

2
pick your battles

One of the most common questions I get is "How do I make sure everything is hot when I serve dinner?" My answer is always: You don't. Trying to make sure everything is piping-hot is a fool's errand, and one I refuse to participate in. Unless you're living an exclusively soup-and-stew lifestyle, there is no reason every dish on your table needs to be hot. If you are serving a pasta that should be, then guess what, you're getting a side of blanched and room-temp broccoli. If that stewed pork with kimchi needs to be piping-hot, then everything else has been made hours ago and stored in the fridge, probably. Pick your battles. Serving different foods that all need to be hot at the same time should not be one of them.

3
never apologize

Having people over means never having to say you're sorry. Not for your mismatched plates or the fact that you don't own any "real" wineglasses or the fact that dinner is actually being served closer to 9:30 than the hoped-for 7:30 (just make sure there are snacks). Embrace the quirky imperfections that make dinner at your house special and different. It's not a restaurant—you shouldn't feel pressure to make it feel like one.

before you begin

shopping

I love grocery shopping the way some people love, say, clothes shopping, and not just because I am particular about the shape of my parsley leaves and the brands of my coconut milk, but because that's when I find unexpected inspiration. How will I know what's out there if I'm not constantly perusing brightly lit aisles, pleasingly organized shelves, chaotic piles of vegetables, and expertly arranged cases of meat? Allowing yourself time to aimlessly wander markets is a necessary experience for creativity in the kitchen—if you're only ever shopping for what you know, how will you ever discover the things you don't?

I shop pretty much everywhere. I love a farmers' market as much as the next gal, and in my fantasy life, I'm there daily, thoughtfully caressing each tomato until I find "the one." But that is not my reality. (I do love New York City's farmers' markets, but getting through a subway turnstile and riding a crowded train with produce for fourteen people is not a chill experience.)

Luckily, most cities and towns have every type of grocery experience you could ever ask for—small neighborhood stores, impressively well-stocked bodegas, specialty spice shops, well-curated fish markets, giant chains, and very small butchers—and I do them all. I shop in Chinatown because they have the best, cheapest produce and I shop in Brighton Beach because they have an insane selection of sour cream and affordable caviar. I shop at farmers' markets because I adore lovingly grown specialty and hyper-seasonal produce (and it's important to support the hard work of small farms), and I cruise giant big-name chains because sometimes that's the only place to find Nilla Wafers.

If you, like me, have a fetish for seasonal produce and an enthusiasm for Eastern European dairy products, then you will agree that searching near and far for new things to bring into your kitchen is a total joy. But if that is not your joy or you simply do not have the time to run all over town, know that nearly everything I use in this book can be found close to home. Everything else can be ordered online.

ingredients

I don't love getting too specific when it comes to brands of ingredients (because not everything is available everywhere) unless I think it really, truly matters, and then I will give you specifics. However, here are a few particular things to keep in mind as you shop for the recipes in this book:

All **salt** for seasoning and baking is kosher (Diamond Crystal is my preferred brand); salt for finishing and garnishing is flaky (I like Jacobsen).

Black pepper is freshly (and preferably coarsely) ground from a pepper mill, never pre-ground.

Olive oil is not the fanciest or the cheapest; make sure it's something you wouldn't mind licking from a spoon.

All **herbs** are fresh unless otherwise noted. For leafy herbs, such as parsley, cilantro, dill, and tarragon, I always include the tender stems along with the leaves (especially when everything's getting all chopped up anyway). For heartier, woody-stemmed herbs such as rosemary, thyme, oregano, and marjoram, I strip the leaves from the stem or leave the sprigs whole if I plan on removing them later.

Red pepper flakes can mean a few different things and, unless specified, I like to leave things open to availability and heat preference. Crushed red pepper flakes are some of the spiciest and most widely available. (This is what you shake on top of pizza.) Other types of crushed red pepper flakes include **Aleppo-style pepper** and **Gochugaru** a.k.a. **Korean chili flakes** (both tend to be sweet, mild and fruity) and **Urfa** (smoky and earthy with little to no heat).

I prefer fresh and coarse **bread crumbs**, but you can almost always use panko as an alternative. I will never suggest using the super-fine sandy variety, which I find nearly useless. **To make your own:** Tear or cut any fresh or stale loaf of crusty bread into 1-inch pieces (I leave the crust on) and pulse in a food processor until you've got tiny, coarse crumbs (no smaller than a grain of rice, no larger than a pea). You can refrigerate or freeze them until needed.

All **nuts** are toasted unless otherwise noted. **To toast:** Place raw nuts on a rimmed baking sheet in a 350°F oven until golden brown and fragrant, smelling almost like popcorn, 6 to 12 minutes depending on the nut.

Buttermilk is always annoyingly labeled "low-fat" or "reduced fat" (1½–2%), which is actually the only buttermilk commercially available. Go for the 2% when you can.

Butter is unsalted unless otherwise noted. The higher the fat percentage, the better.

All **cheese**, from parmesan to cheddar, is from a hunk and never pre-grated or shredded because there are anti-caking (and occasionally anti-aging) agents added, which change the flavor and texture of the cheese.

equipment

I live in a place where space is sacred and scarce. I favor my same six-year-old sheet pans and ancient cast-iron skillets. I own only kitchen tools that I find indispensable. I am a Luddite and resist technology at every turn, and no place more so than the kitchen. Here is my basic list of tools I cannot live without. (I find other items, such as food processors, stand mixers, and grills, to be selectively useful but not desert-island worthy.)

Stainless-steel skillets. Knock yourself out with as many as you want, but I pretty much use only two: one large (10 to 12 inches), one small (6 to 8 inches).

Large Dutch oven. They don't come in standard sizes, but you'll definitely want one in the 7- to 8-quart range. Anything larger is kind of overkill for the average household, and anything smaller is no doubt fun and generally useful but not large enough to hold, say, a 5-pound pork shoulder.

Rimmed baking sheets. I use these to roast on and bake in, of course, but have also found them to be super useful in kitchen organization (I keep one in my refrigerator for leaky or sticky condiments and one on wire shelving for stable open-pantry storage) and have even used them as a serving tray when necessary.

Microplane. For finely grating citrus, cheese, and garlic, my three favorite ingredients.

Peeler. The cheap plastic Y peeler is truly the best. I own several in many colors (since I always seem to be misplacing them and, hey, they are very affordable). No other peeler comes close to doing as good a job.

Wooden spoon, silicone or rubber spatula, metal whisk. The trifecta of common kitchen tools, indispensable for cooking and baking. I prefer the most basic versions of all of these.

Fish spatula. The flexible, perforated spatula is useful for so many things beyond what the name would suggest. Use to toss roasted vegetables, flip an egg, or transfer a cake to a plate or chicken to a platter.

Metal tongs. These should always be metal tipped and cheap. (I find the best ones available at restaurant supply stores.) They are essentially an extension of my hand when I cook, and I am constantly using them in lieu of a spoon or spatula to flip, turn, pick up, stir, and transfer.

pantry essentials

A well-stocked pantry (and refrigerator) will save your life. Once you've got things like olive oil, salt, and pepper, there are other big-ticket items that are great for keeping around the house. They will always prove helpful when having people over. Here is an inexhaustive list of some of the things I keep on hand.

Cheese! Hard, aged cheeses like parmesan and pecorino. Not only are they good for your own personal hunger emergencies, but they are also great because they last forever. Seriously,

I probably have some aged parmesan from two years ago in my fridge *right now*. And guess what? I am absolutely going to serve it to you.

Aside from casual snacking and impromptu cheese plates, a grating of parm or pec atop a bowl of grains, pasta, roasted vegetables, or salad is always welcome. I like to serve a hunk of it on a plate with a microplane, peeler, or other grating tool so people can DIT (Do It Themselves).

Tinned fish. In many parts of the world, tinned fish is a common and expected snack, but here in the United States of I Don't Like Tinned Fish, it can be a harder sell. Nevertheless, I have been known to open a can and set it out for snack time, or include it alongside other things like crushed potato salad (page 135) or seafood pasta (page 250) where those fishies are good in, on, and with. For more on my favorite tinned fish, the best ways to serve it, and what to serve it with, check out the exclusive invitation to the Fish Party on page 38.

Tangy, briny things. Pickles, olives, capers, caper berries, pearl onions, and the like have their own shelf in my refrigerator. Of course, I use them to cook with and to set out at dinnertime as part of a spread, but more often than not, I'm using them to feature prominently in any and all of my snacking scenarios. Even if you have "nothing" in your fridge, when you set out a bowl of olives (better yet, Fancy Citrusy Olives, page 59, people will think you are an excellent, extremely put-together host.

Crackers. I was originally going to do a ranking of store-bought crackers, but then realized I enjoy being likable and do not want the majority of people reading this book to burn it when they discover I prefer Triscuits to Ritz. But whatever your cracker truth is, whether it's buttery or wheaty, studded with dried cranberries or topped with rosemary, live it large. In case you haven't heard, crackers are good with cheese (page 45), but also with tinned fish (page 29) and every single dip in this world (and in this book). They are good on their own out of the box in the middle of the night and they are good topped with sour cream and a spoonful of caviar at your next festive gathering. Crackers truly live that high/low life, and for that virtue alone, they have earned a permanent position in my pantry.

Citrus. I haven't done the exact math, but I'd say 90 percent of the recipes in this book encourage or require the use of citrus. Maybe it's the peel for your DIY martini bar (page 63), or maybe I want you to chop up a whole lemon for a salad dressing (page 87), but whatever the case, lemons, limes, oranges, and grapefruits breathe life into nearly everything they touch. For the recipes alone they're all worth having on hand, but also know a bowl of tangerines make a very acceptable last-minute (and delightfully phoned-in) dessert.

Seltzer. Imagine how excited you get when you're at a restaurant that offers complimentary sparkling water? This is how your friends will feel when they know you've got an abundance of seltzer waiting for them. Maybe I've been in New York too long (seltzer capital of the world, baby!), but I can't imagine not having it around. It's great for mixing (preferably for A Very Fine Spritz, page 33), for hydrating (right?), for sipping in between too much wine. Doesn't matter if it comes from a can, bottle, or a home machine, it's a nice touch. Bonus points if you give it a twist of citrus. So classy!

A loaf of bread. Whenever I buy fresh bread, I'll often freeze at least half the loaf for later use. "Later use," in many cases turns out to be when people come over and I realize that I either forgot to buy bread or ran out of bread or panic that I didn't make enough food and three extra

people showed up and you know what is good and filling? Bread.

Not for nothing, it's also good for croutons (page 77) and bread crumbs (page 14) which hopefully you'll be making a lot of once you read this book.

To rejuvenate kind-of-stale or refrigerated bread: Preheat the oven to 450°F. Quickly run the whole loaf of bread under running water just to barely soak the crust. Place it directly on the wire rack in the oven and bake until the crust is once again toasty and crunchy and the inside is warmed and fluffy, 10 to 15 minutes. Serve whole, slice it, or tear it.

For frozen bread: Preheat the oven to 450°F. Wrap the bread in aluminum foil and bake 10 to 15 minutes, just to take the edge off. Remove the bread from the foil and follow the instructions above.

Chocolate. Chocolate and I are not best friends—rather, we're acquaintances who share close mutual friends. Without fail, at least one person I invite over will always ask if I have "a little something chocolatey," and who am I to deny them? So I keep small bars of high-quality chocolate or cookies like chocolate Pocky or wafers on hand to satisfy them. (For a more DIY tiny chocolate experience, there are cookies on page 306.)

Vanilla ice cream. Not to sound vanilla, but vanilla ice cream is the best ice cream. It is the only flavor that goes with absolutely everything, and for that I value it above all others. I like to think of it as whipped cream but better and you didn't even have to do anything. Hibiscus-Roasted Peaches (page 304)? Vanilla ice cream. Lemony Turmeric Tea Cake (page 309)? Really great with vanilla ice cream. Crispy Chocolate Cake (page 288)? YES, VANILLA ICE CREAM, PLEASE. If you're having people over, just buy some and you'll find a use for it, even if you weren't even planning on making dessert (page 271). You won't be sorry.

snack
time

Do not confuse snacks with hors d'oeuvres or canapés.

I would never use either of those terms. Snacks are not stressful art projects—snacks are breezy, snacks are fun. Snacks are a delicious diversion, a class of foods to mitigate the stress of realizing at 7:30 your dinner won't be ready for another two hours. You will not find elaborate mini sandwiches for twenty or anything in a blanket (sorry) in this chapter. What you WILL find are easy-ish and extremely delicious and very addicting little somethings to, uh, snack on, while you wait for the main event. Or maybe snacks *are* the main event, who could say?

This section includes what I consider to be snack essentials (which could also double as my favorite food groups). There are creamy dips, spicy nuts, salted fruits, tangy vegetables, and, of course, so much cheese. There are recipe-recipes and more ideas for things that you can just throw together. There's even an entire spread predicated on your accepting smoked and tinned fish into your heart, plus a (quick-rising!) focaccia that you (yes, you!) can bake. Tonight. Welcome to my snack party, where there's no assembly required, toothpicks are optional, and dreams come true.

Labne with Sizzled Scallions and Chile (Almost Ranch)

makes 2 cups

⅓ cup olive oil

4 scallions (or green garlic), white and light green parts, thinly sliced

1 teaspoon crushed red pepper flakes

2 tablespoons finely chopped fresh cilantro (tender leaves and stems) or chives, plus more for garnish

Flaky sea salt

Freshly ground black pepper

2 cups labne, full-fat Greek yogurt, or sour cream

2 tablespoons fresh lemon juice

Among some of my friends, this has become known as "The Dip," and now I literally cannot attend any social gathering or host any dinner party without someone requesting "The Dip." When you make it, you'll know why. It's my very high-brow version of ranch dressing, and that's all the intel you need. But if you'd like to know more, there is a scalliony chile oil that gets sizzled with cilantro stems (or chives) and swirled into thick, lemony labne. From there, I'm sure you can assume that the combination of tangy dairy coupled with that herby chile oil already sounds incredible, and maybe you are on your way to making this right now. If you can find green garlic (which tends to be hyper-seasonal and mostly found only at farmers' markets), use them (or even ramps!) in place of the scallions.

1 Heat the olive oil, scallions, crushed red pepper flakes, and cilantro in a small pot over medium-low heat. Cook, swirling occasionally, until the scallions and red pepper flakes start to visually and audibly sizzle and frizzle and turn the oil a bright fiery orange. Remove from the heat and let cool enough to taste without burning your mouth, then season with salt and pepper.

2 Combine the labne and lemon juice in a medium bowl and season with salt and pepper. Spoon into a bowl and swirl in the sizzled scallion mixture. Top with extra cilantro, if you like.

DO AHEAD Sizzled scallion oil can be made up to a week ahead, wrapped tightly, and refrigerated. Labne can be seasoned 1 week ahead, wrapped tightly, and refrigerated. Combine the two just before serving.

Garlicky Beet Dip with Walnuts

makes about 2 cups

1 pound beets or carrots, tops removed and scrubbed, or sweet potatoes

⅓ cup olive oil, plus more for drizzling

Kosher salt and freshly ground black pepper

1 garlic clove, finely grated

⅓ cup walnuts, hazelnuts, or almonds, toasted (see page 14)

2 tablespoons red wine vinegar or white wine vinegar, plus more as needed

½ cup sour cream or full-fat Greek yogurt (optional)

¼ cup fresh dill, coarsely chopped

NOTE *Traditionally made with roasted red peppers and sometimes tomato, romesco is a tangy, lightly spiced, nutty saucy spread. It's good as a dip for raw vegetables, but also as a spread for things like "stuff on crackers" and also "stuff on toast"—which, yes, can also mean it's good on a sandwich, but there are no sandwiches in this book. Sorry.*

Here, roasted beets take the place of the roasted red peppers in this romesco-esque dip. (I have a very inflexible "no bell pepper" policy.) But it's also a concept so versatile that it's definitely worth exploring with different roasted vegetables. I can give you a head start and tell you that roasted carrots, sweet potatoes, and eggplant are all winners. This version, which is in no way authentically representing *romesco* (just inspired by it!), doesn't have any spices added, since I find the raw garlickyness and the sweetness of the beets to be interesting enough; but ground turmeric, ground cumin, and paprika would all work here. Beets always need a bit of tangy fattiness to counter their sweetness, so I swirl in a bit of yogurt or sour cream, but that's definitely optional if you're going dairy-free.

1 Preheat the oven to 425°F.

2 Place the beets in a large baking dish. Drizzle with olive oil and season with salt and pepper. Roast until totally and completely fork-tender, 60 to 70 minutes, depending on size. (If you're doing this with sweet potatoes, they'll take about the same amount of time; carrots will take less time—40 to 45 minutes.)

3 Remove from the oven and let cool enough so that you can peel them, then cut into smaller chunks.

4 Place the beets, garlic, nuts, olive oil, and the vinegar in the bowl of a food processor. Pulse until you've got the texture of your dreams, which is different for all of us. For me, it's not perfectly smooth but processed enough to spread. If you like chunkier or smoother, then go for it.

5 Once your desired texture is reached, fold in the sour cream, if using. Season with salt, pepper, and more vinegar. Transfer to your cutest bowl, drizzle with more olive oil, and top with dill.

DO AHEAD Dip can be made up to 1 week ahead, wrapped tightly, and refrigerated.

Creamy Sesame Turmeric Dip

makes about 2 cups

8 ounces cream cheese or ricotta,
    preferably room temperature
¾ cup sour cream or labne
¼ cup tahini
2 tablespoons water
Kosher salt and freshly ground
    pepper
¼ cup olive oil
2 tablespoons white sesame seeds
1 teaspoon ground turmeric
Flaky sea salt

NOTE *This is a rare occurence where I prefer whipped cream cheese to unwhipped cream cheese, because it eliminates the need to use a food processor, but both work.*

Everyone needs a "house snack," meaning a snack that friends can come to expect every time they come over. I have two: parmesan cheese and this dip. The ratio of cream cheese to sour cream changes depending on what I've got on hand, and sometimes I add handfuls of herbs or a pinch of crushed red pepper flakes, whatever. The basic idea is something creamy laced with tahini and swirled with a magic mixture made from toasted sesame, dried turmeric, and so much olive oil. My favorite thing to eat it with is a box of Ak-Mak crackers, but anything you like to dip, please dip away.

1 Combine the cream cheese, sour cream, tahini, and water in the bowl of a food processor. Pulse until well blended and creamy (alternatively, use a fork or spoon; there might just be a few lumps, which is actually fine). Season with salt and pepper.

2 Heat the olive oil and sesame seeds in a small skillet or pot over medium heat. Cook, swirling occasionally, until the sesame seeds are toasted and fragrant, 2 to 3 minutes. Add the turmeric and remove from heat.

3 Transfer the cream cheese mixture to a cute serving bowl and top with the sesame-turmeric oil. Finish with flaky salt and more pepper before serving.

the only fish
in the sea

One of my defining character traits is "loves anchovies," for which I will not apologize. They are meaty, briny, salty, and perfect in every way in nearly any application: in marinades, in salads, in sauces, in stews, and maybe most especially, on their own for snack time. Personal snack, private snack, anywhere in between.

Anchovy fillets come in both jars and tins of varying sizes. Both are great, but in my opinion, unless you're going to be cooking with or eating the whole tin, a jar is more efficient. (My favorite widely available brands are Ortiz and Cento. They are high enough quality to eat raw, and affordable enough to cook with.) When you open the jar or tin, the anchovies should be pink, firm, and have a good, briny, funky smell (just like good cheese, there is a difference between good funky and bad funky—you'll know the difference).

I would happily eat anchovies out of a jar or just smeared onto soft, buttered bread or crunchy, garlicky toast, but one of the most fun ways to eat them is in the style of a "Gilda," a popular Spanish snack in which anchovies are skewered on a toothpick along with spicy pickled peppers or olives or both. Generally, I'm not big on serving things on a toothpick because it makes me feel like I'm catering a wedding, but these snacks are cute and decidedly unfussy to throw together. They're also the perfect thing to ask your friends to do while you prepare everything else for dinner.

Spicy Marinated Anchovies with Potato Chips

serves 4 to 8

1–2 tins or 1 jar of anchovy fillets
¼ cup distilled white vinegar
4 Calabrian chiles, pepperoncini, or guindilla peppers, thinly sliced, or a good pinch of crushed red pepper flakes
Potato chips

NOTE *The potato chip is an extremely personal thing, and I would never force my very high standards and strict opinions on you (just kidding—yes, I would!), but if you're asking me, choose something neutral in flavor and sturdy in texture. Kettle or Cape Cod potato chips are both stellar national brands, but I'd never kick a Ruffles or Lay's out of bed, either. The important thing is that they are not crumbled or crushed—you must have a whole potato chip to fully appreciate this experience, no crumbs allowed.*

I am going to tell you an annoying story: One day, I was having a perfect afternoon in Sicily, drinking a perfect Aperol spritz and eating perfect olives. (I told you this story was annoying.) I was about to order a perfect gelato, but instead, these perfect little anchovies appeared next to a bowl of perfectly salty potato chips. I assumed they were supposed to be eaten together, otherwise why appear together so kismet-like? Anyway, I'm not sure if they were or not, because I didn't see anyone else topping chips with anchovies, but that really doesn't matter because they were perfect together. I promise this story will be at least 80 percent less irritating once you've made these for yourself.

1 Open up your tin(s) or jar of anchovies and drain them of the oil. Transfer the anchovies to a cute plate or shallow bowl and cover with the vinegar.

2 Scatter the chiles over the anchovies. The point is to make 'em spicy. Let them sit like this for at least 10 minutes, and up to 1 hour ahead.

3 Eat the anchovies on potato chips, like an American tourist in Italy. Aperol spritzes are optional but recommended.

a very
fine spritz

I am a huge fan of the spritz—Aperol spritzes, Campari spritzes, Cappelletti spritzes, white wine spritzes; basically anything that can be spritzed, I'll spritz it. I prefer to think of the low-ABV spritz as a light, easy refreshment rather than "a cocktail." This allows me to drink several over the course of many hours without getting unreasonably drunk. Ditching the word *cocktail* also allows me to use a ratio, not a recipe. (No disrespect to spritz recipes, but let's just say that in no universe am I busting out a small measuring cup to make a cocktail as casual as this.) Looking and tasting like a fantasy vacation, spritzes are universally appealing and bring joy to everyone who is lucky enough to be drinking one.

There are many ways to make one of these delightfully effervescent beverages, and I don't think anyone should feel hemmed in by exact measurements or specific ingredients. My most basic version involves a third sweet-bitter liquor (such as Aperol, Campari, Cappelletti, Lillet, or Suze—there are lots out there, so feel free to experiment), a third sparkling or even regular wine (while I don't encourage the drinking of sub-par wine, this is actually a good time to use a bottle of sub-par wine), and a third soda water (seltzer or club soda). Keep in mind that these ratios will not be the same depending on where you go and who you ask, but this is a good place to start.

TO MAKE

Fill a large glass of your choosing (rocks glass, wineglass, highball glass, anything goes!) with ice. Fill it one third of the way with a sweet-bitter liquor, such as **Aperol, Campari, Cappelletti, Lillet,** or **Suze**. From here, top with one third **sparkling wine** or regular **white wine** or **rosé**, and then top the remaining third with **soda water**. Garnish with a **lemon, orange,** or **grapefruit** slice, wedge, or peel. Now go forth and spritz away into the night (or day)!

Any Excuse to Make Shrimp Cocktail

serves 6 to 10

FOR THE SAUCE

2 cups Heinz ketchup

¼ cup fresh lemon juice, plus more to taste

3 tablespoons yuzu kosho or harissa paste, plus more to taste

1 tablespoon Worcestershire or Maggi sauce

Kosher salt and freshly ground black pepper

Freshly grated or prepared horseradish (if you must)

FOR THE SHRIMP

2–3 pounds large raw, unpeeled shrimp

Kosher salt

1 large onion, quartered

A handful of black peppercorns

3 lemons, 1 halved crosswise and 2 quartered

Olives or cornichons (optional)

Lemony Aioli (recipe follows, optional)

NOTE *Heinz ketchup is the only brand of ketchup I recognize.*

You know those people at a party who stand by the shrimp cocktail platter and not so secretly eat pretty much the whole platter, hoping nobody notices but also not caring enough to stop? That is 100 percent me at every party. That's why I've decided that I will no longer wait for a holiday or somebody's birthday so I can eat endless shrimp cocktail. I will throw my *own* party, for which I will poach my own shrimp and make my own cocktail sauce, and eat half of it myself, probably. There doesn't need to be an occasion, reason or excuse to do this. Or perhaps you do, and the reason is "I feel like eating a lot of shrimp cocktail tonight," and that will be good enough.

As for the sauces, I like *my* cocktail sauce on the spicy, lemony side, but it's up to you how lemony or spicy your personal cocktail sauce is. I'm also not one of those people who *have* to have horseradish in their cocktail sauce, but if you feel passionately about this, go on ahead and add it. Aioli is not classically involved in shrimp cocktail, but to me the more dips in any given situation, the better. Mayonnaise doctored with lots of lemon and raw garlic will also do the trick.

1 Make the sauce. Combine the ketchup, ¼ cup lemon juice, yuzu kosho, and Worcestershire sauce in a medium bowl. Season with salt, pepper, and more lemon juice, if you like. If you're a real purist, go ahead and add a spoonful or two of horseradish, or simply season with more yuzu kosho. Set aside to serve with the shrimp, or eat shamelessly with a spoon.

2 Prepare the shrimp. Peel but do not devein the shrimp (otherwise they will get all curly when they cook). If the idea of eating undeveined shrimp really, really bothers you, go ahead and devein them, but it's really not a big deal, I promise!

3 Bring a large pot of highly salted (salty like the sea!) water to a boil and add the onion and peppercorns. Working in batches as needed, lower the shrimp into the pot and cook just until they're bright pink and opaque, 3 to 4 minutes. Drain or remove using a slotted spoon and transfer to a rimmed baking sheet so they can cool down as quickly as possible. (Should you miraculously have space in your refrigerator, place them in there to chill faster.) Continue to cook the shrimp, as needed.

4 To serve: Squeeze some of the halved lemon over the shrimp. Fill a large bowl with ice and then place shrimp atop with the lemon wedges; there's no need to arrange them concentrically or anything, just however you think looks nice. If desired, scatter a few olives or tiny cornichons onto the ice as well. Be sure to provide a little dish for tails.

5 Serve with cocktail sauce and lemony aioli for dipping.

DO AHEAD Cocktail sauce can be made 2 weeks ahead, but honestly if you're prepping food for a party 2 weeks ahead, you should relax a little!

Lemony Aioli

makes 2 cups

2 large egg yolks
2 teaspoons fresh lemon juice, plus
  more as necessary
Kosher salt
½ cup olive oil
½ cup grapeseed or vegetable oil
1 small garlic clove, finely grated
  (optional)
1 tablespoon finely grated lemon
  zest (optional)

1 Whisk the egg yolks, lemon juice, and a pinch of salt together in a medium bowl (one that is deeper than it is wide, if possible—it's easier to emulsify everything together when it's concentrated in one area). Combine both oils together in a measuring cup with a spout.

2 In a slow, steady stream, add the oil mixture to the egg mixture, 1 tablespoon at a time, whisking all along, making sure whatever you've added is completely incorporated before whisking more oil in. Continue with all the oil, thinning with water or lemon juice as needed to keep the future aioli from becoming too thick. (The ideal thickness is extremely personal, but when you know, you know.)

3 Whisk in the garlic and lemon zest, if using, and season with more salt and lemon juice as desired.

fish for days

Smoked and tinned fish is a thing that I will happily buy because the quality of what you can purchase from places and people who do it expertly is very high. But sure, aside from bringing a whole smoked trout to your friends as a housewarming gift (a thing I have done!), how best to enjoy it?

Well, to properly have what can be described as an excellent Fish Party, there are a few key elements that must be included. It's a bit of an *If You Give a Mouse a Cookie* situation in that if you're going to have a Fish Party . . .

Then you'll need to get some fish. Assuming you're not hopping a plane to Portugal to go grocery shopping, there are plenty of specialty stores with wide selections and chain grocery stores with at least a selection, which counts for something. "Fish" here does also not need to be limited to specifically fish, in that fish eggs like cured salmon or trout roe and tinned shellfish like razor clams and mussels are also welcome to attend this soiree. Experiment with different brands and types until you find the one that speaks to you. (Spicy mackerel with piquillo peppers from Spain! Sardines in olive oil from Italy! Smoked salmon from Manhattan's Lower East Side!) When it comes to most things, I don't think that more expensive translates to higher quality, but with tinned and smoked fish, I do believe there is a correlation and it might be a good time to splurge.

And if you have all this fish, you'll need something to put it on. Large, sturdy crackers are always my choice since they aren't too bready but can still hold up to a pile o' fish and can be picked up without collapse. If you are going to do bread, I recommend choosing a seedy, dense rye or something else dense and a little textured, slicing it thin and toasting it well. I know others who like a thick, toasty slice from a boule or baguette, but to me that is more "Toast with Fish," and this is not that, so . . .

And if you have salty, fatty fish on a cracker, you'll need something tangy, spicy, or both to cut through that salty fattiness. This list can get kind of long, so I'll give you my greatest hits: Thinly sliced **raw onion** for its savory punchiness, **pickled pearl onions** and **cornichons** for tang. **Caper berries** for their delightfully textured seedy insides and clean brininess. **Fresh herbs**, specifically **dill**, **chives**, and **parsley**. **Calabrian chiles** or **pickled peppers** like **guindillas** or **peperoncini** for that heat I know you want.

And if you have all that freshness and tanginess, you'll need something creamy and rich to balance it all out. **Softened butter** with flaky salt, bowls of **sour cream** or **labne** seasoned with lemon, and/or (preferably *and*) **garlicky aioli** or **mayonnaise** would all be great. The **yolks of good jammy eggs**, while not technically a spoonable situation like the others, would also do a good job of providing luscious sauciness, and so I often set out a few halved soft- or medium-boiled eggs for topping or nibbling alongside.

Smashed Eggs and Fancy Fish on Crackers

serves 6 to 12

6–12 large eggs
Lemony Aioli (page 37), mayonnaise, full-fat Greek yogurt, crème fraîche, or sour cream
Crackers or well-toasted toast
Finely chopped fresh chives
Coarsely chopped fresh dill
Coarsely chopped fresh parsley
Flaky sea salt and coarsely ground black pepper
Smoked trout or salmon, or other tinned, smoked, or cured fish
Caper berries and/or cornichons, halved
1 lemon, quartered, for serving
Sliced red onion, for serving (optional)

NOTE *This is the kind of snack I would rather not assemble for someone else. Not to be rude, but if you're coming over, I am already doing a lot of work and I don't feel like I need to assemble a cracker for you. I put all the stuff out so nicely! Isn't that enough? But if you are a more generous and kind host than I am, feel free.*

Smashing eggs onto crackers might seem like a thing you'd make for breakfast, and you're not wrong—I eat that for breakfast a lot. But when the eggs (specifically, just cooked, jammy eggs) are dressed up with something creamy, lots of herbs, and whatever cured, tinned, or smoked fish you may have on hand (you have all of that on hand, right?), and maybe some pickles or caper berries, it's also a really great pre-dinner, cocktail hour, or maybe we're-having-snacks-for-dinner meal.

1 Bring a medium pot of water to a boil. Gently lower the eggs into the pot and boil for 6 minutes. SIX MINUTES. Not a minute more, not a minute less.

2 Transfer the eggs to a bowl and run cold water over them. The nice thing about this 6-minute cook time is that it allows for a bit of carryover, so that if you don't have an ice bath (I never do), the yolks will still be perfectly jammy with just the right amount of runniness. If you're worried, know that here it is better to have the eggs slightly over than under to avoid a huge yolk-y mess on your hands.

3 Peel the eggs, put them in a festive dish or bowl, and set them on a table with all the remaining ingredients, which are accoutrements for personalized smashing and assembly. It's fairly intuitive, but if anyone needs guidance, you can direct them thus:

"If you want aioli, sour cream, mayonnaise, or whatever, spread a bit of that onto your cracker or toast of choice. Then, split an egg with a knife or use a fork and smash it onto the cracker. Top with any combination of fish, chives, dill, parsley, flaky salt, pepper, caper berries, cornichons, and/or red onions. Here are lemon wedges for squeezing over. Please enjoy."

Trout Roe on Buttered Toast with Lemony Herbs

serves as many as you need it to

Good bread, preferably rye, sliced
    about ⅛–¼ inch thick, toasted
Plenty of good-quality salted or
    unsalted butter, softened
Flaky sea salt and coarsely cracked
    black pepper
1 (2-ounce) jar trout or salmon roe
    (smoked or unsmoked)
Coarsely chopped fresh chives,
    parsley and/or dill, tender leaves
    and stems
Lemon, for zesting

NOTE *Smoked salmon, gravlax, and other tinned fish are good here, too.*

You don't need me to tell you that buttered toast is good, but maybe you need me to tell you that buttered toast with tiny, smoky, salty beads of trout roe is magnificent. To me, trout roe is like a more flavorful, prettier caviar. It isn't the cheapest thing in this book, but the lesson here is that you can pull out exactly one stop and people will be impressed (that stop is, of course, the trout roe). This is the type of snack you can certainly assemble for others, but I prefer to simply set everything out and let people make their own little toasts.

1 Slather the bread with some of the butter. If there was ever a time to use the phrase "Don't be shy," this would be it. Don't be shy with the butter! Sprinkle with salt and pepper.

2 Delicately and confidently spoon the roe onto the bread. Scatter with the herbs, add lemon zest, and serve.

a better
cheese plate

As anyone who has ever thrown or attended any sort of party or gathering knows, the most important thing is not the wine, what you've decided to wear, or the playlist you spent hours preparing. It's the cheese. Even more important than dip, a solid cheese presence will soften the awkward conversation that happens when the only two people who don't know each other get to the party first. It will nourish the bodies of every person who arrives with an empty stomach, and if they are my friends, that will be every person you invited. It will feed the party long into the evening when everything takes longer to cook than you thought it would. A good cheese plate will buy you time when you need it, and for that, it is truly invaluable.

The cheese plate is not a contest to see how many different types of cheese you can find. In my opinion, it's better to have a larger quantity of three very different, very good cheeses (i.e., one firm and salty, another semi-soft and peppery, the other soft and creamy) rather than smaller quantities of many mediocre varieties. I prefer crackers to bread or toast, but having both on hand is not a bad idea.

When it comes to presentation, my only word of advice is: Please relax. Unless you're styling a mail-order catalog for monogrammed plaid picnic sets, you can skip the fanned slices and adorably bunched grapes. In fact, if you want to skip the preslicing altogether, setting out a small knife (or small spoon, should you be blessed with a creamy enough cheese) for each cheese is a good idea. As for what to serve it on, you don't need to source a reclaimed slab of plywood or dig out the perfect slate from a nearby quarry—a large cutting board, regular platter, or even plastic serving tray are all wonderful options.

For smaller gatherings (two to six people), I love to pick one kind of cheese and really lean into it, such as placing a hunk of very good parmesan on a plate, sticking a knife into it, and urging friends to break off little nibbles for themselves. If anyone seems confused or complains about this, tell them, "That's how they do it in Italy," even if that's only partly true.

If you want to do more of a "composed cheese" vibe, a nice thing to do is slice thin pieces of a firm, salty cheese and layer them with thinly sliced vegetables tossed in vinegar or lemon juice, or with spicy, jammy fruit, or a with a drizzle of something like maple syrup. Drizzle everything with olive oil and give it a sprinkle of something like black pepper, sumac, or crushed red pepper flakes. Some nice combos to get you started are **parmesan** (king of cheese) and **radishes tossed in vinegar**, sliced or crumbled **Gouda** (queen of cheese) drizzled with **maple syrup or honey** and an extremely good dose of **crushed black pepper**, or slices of a salty, **semi-soft sheep's-milk cheese** (also cheese royalty) served with **fresh apricots** that have been crushed with a bit of **sugar and fresh or dried chili**.

Spicy Tomato-Marinated Feta

serves 6 to 8

½ cup olive oil, plus more as needed

2 garlic cloves, thinly sliced

2 small-ish (or 1 medium) ripe tomatoes (4 to 6 ounces total), coarsely chopped

Kosher salt and freshly ground black pepper

2 tablespoons harissa paste, or ½ teaspoon crushed red pepper flakes

1 tablespoon distilled white vinegar

8 ounces feta cheese, sliced into ¼-inch slabs or ½-inch cubes

This one goes out to the cheese guy at Sahadi's, my favorite grocery store in all of Brooklyn. He knows everything about all the cheeses but seems to have a special fondness for the vast feta selection. All these giant glistening white cubes of cheese sitting in a jar of brine, ready to be cut for you *to order* behind his little cheese counter, which is just so charmingly old-school it almost makes me forget that things like the internet exist.

My guy will explain to you that he loves to experiment with different marinades for his feta, which he occasionally sells. I find all of them delightfully delicious, but my favorite one has a million different red pepper flakes in it along with the harissa and sun-dried tomatoes. This is my tribute, using fewer ingredients and fresh tomatoes instead of dried for extra sauciness.

You can eat this cheese spooned onto crackers, picked up with a small fork, and so on. Spread onto toast, it doesn't not taste like pizza, just saying.

1 Heat the olive oil in a medium skillet over medium heat. Add the garlic and cook, swirling the skillet occasionally, until the garlic is tender and nearly golden brown, 2 to 3 minutes.

2 Add the tomatoes and season with salt and pepper. Cook, stirring occasionally, until they've broken down into a thick, chunky sauce, 5 to 8 minutes.

3 Add the harissa and continue to cook until the sauce is a bit more paste-like, another 3 to 5 minutes. Remove from the heat, then add the vinegar and season with salt and pepper. Add more olive oil until it becomes savory and spoonable.

4 Place the feta in a serving dish or bowl and pour the tomato mixture over. Let sit at least 10 minutes, or up to a week in advance, refrigerated. Drizzle with more olive oil before serving.

DO AHEAD Feta can be marinated up to 1 week ahead, tightly wrapped, and refrigerated.

Crispy Haloumi with Honey and Pistachio

serves 4 to 6

8 ounces haloumi or queso fresco,
    sliced into ½-inch slabs
2 tablespoons honey
2 tablespoons finely chopped
    toasted pistachios (see page 14)
Flaky sea salt

Think of this as the opposite of fondue, wherein the objective isn't to melt the cheese but, rather, to brown it, crisping it while caramelizing the milk solids, which gives it a "cheese that stuck to the side of the pan when making a grilled cheese" effect. Coupled with some sweet honey and salty, crunchy pistachios, well, this is what one might call "a real crowd pleaser."

While it's great even at room temperature, this is one of the few fussy-ish things in this chapter that's best eaten warm and preferably, right off the pan.

1 Heat a well-seasoned cast-iron or nonstick skillet over medium-high heat (you don't need oil). Working with a few batches at a time, sear the cheese on one side until it's golden brown (it won't melt, just brown), almost like you're searing a steak, 3 to 5 minutes. Flip and repeat on the other side. Remove and place on a plate. Continue with the remaining cheese.

2 Drizzle the cheese with the honey and sprinkle with the pistachios and flaky salt. This doesn't *have* to be served warm, but at the very least, cut yourself a piece before serving it to others—you know, just to try. To me, this is very much a food to be eaten with hands, but if you want to use toothpicks or small forks, that is okay, too.

Your Very Own Marinated Artichoke Hearts

serves 6 to 8

½ cup olive oil

2 sprigs fresh oregano

1 lemon, thinly sliced, seeds removed

1 shallot, thinly sliced

Kosher salt and freshly ground black pepper

2 (14–ounce) cans artichoke hearts in water, drained, halved or quartered

2 tablespoons white wine vinegar

½ cup fresh mint or parsley leaves

NOTE *I rarely prefer things from a can or a jar when they can be found fresh, but there are a few exceptions, like chickpeas and artichoke hearts. Fresh artichokes are genuinely a true gift, but trimming and turning a raw artichoke to get to the heart is not what I'd call an easy process. The good news is that you can buy them in a jar or can, and they are very good!*

With artichoke hearts, I want to eat as many as possible in one sitting, but the store-bought marinated ones are actually too tangy to do this. If you feel me on that, then you will be pleased to know that non-marinated artichoke hearts are just as easy to purchase as the marinated variety and that means you can just . . . marinate them yourself! This way, you control the flavors and ingredients, the level of acidity, the saltiness, the everything. I like mine to taste like they've been bathing in Italian dressing from a bottle with Paul Newman's face on it, with lots of fresh oregano and thinly sliced shallot. Feel free to customize the marinade with various herbs and alliums, adding more or less vinegar depending on your preference, but I would not advise skipping the lemon because I feel that you'd really miss it.

I will happily eat these all on their own, pierced with a tiny fork or toothpick in between bites of hard, salty cheese or maybe very thin slices of cured meat, but they also make an excellent topper for long, thin crackers like carta di musica or thick pieces of toast smeared with a creamy cheese. You can also set them out as part of your not-crudité platter (page 54); anything goes!

1 Heat the olive oil, oregano, lemon slices, and shallot in a medium skillet over medium heat. Cook, swirling occasionally, until the shallot and lemon start to sizzle and brown a bit, 4 to 6 minutes. Season with salt and pepper and remove from heat.

2 Place the artichoke hearts in a medium bowl and pour the oil mixture on top, followed by the vinegar. Season again with salt and pepper and let sit at least 30 minutes.

3 Just before serving, transfer to a serving dish or bowl and scatter with the mint.

DO AHEAD Artichoke hearts can be marinated for up to 2 weeks ahead (without the herbs), tightly sealed, and stored in the refrigerator.

Creamy Goat Cheese with Lemony Za'atar

serves 6 to 8

2 tablespoons white sesame seeds

½ cup olive oil, plus more for
  drizzling

½ lemon (peel, pith, and all), seeds
  removed, finely chopped

2 teaspoons ground sumac, plus
  more for serving

1 tablespoon fresh thyme, chopped,
  plus more for serving

Kosher salt and freshly ground black
  pepper

8 ounces fresh goat cheese,
  coarsely crumbled

Crackers or toast, for serving

I love a good, creamy goat cheese. You know who else loves it? Probably everyone you know. Is creamy goat cheese "cool?" No, but I can't be bothered to care. Make your friends admit they like it again by crumbling it into a cute dish, drizzling it with a lemony sesame seed mixture and sprinkling it with lots of sumac. They will ask, "Is this from the newest casual Mediterranean small plates hotspot?" and you'll reply, "Yes, it's called chèvre."

1 Toast the sesame seeds in a small skillet over medium heat until golden brown and smelling like toasted sesame, 2 to 3 minutes. Add the olive oil, lemon, sumac, and thyme, swirling to get everything submerged in the oil. Season with salt and pepper and let gently simmer a minute or two for maximum infusion. Remove from heat and let sit another minute or two.

2 Place the goat cheese in a small dish, glass jar, or other container. Pour the olive oil mixture over and let sit at least 10 minutes, drizzling with more olive oil as needed to kind of submerge slightly (the oil is part of the eating experience and should be spooned onto the cracker or toast as well).

3 To serve, finish with a bit more fresh thyme and a sprinkle of sumac and set out with crackers or slices of toast.

DO AHEAD Goat cheese can be marinated up to a week ahead, wrapped tightly, and refrigerated.

don't call it
a crudité

My earliest memory of what I now know as "crudités" is the platter of vegetables my grandma would put out for company on holidays. She would pull out every stop imaginable, spending what felt like hours on each vegetable, carving the radishes into tulips, making crookneck squash into geese by placing toothpicks under the bulb to act as legs and sticking black peppercorns into the top to make eyes (creepy, in retrospect), trimming away 80 percent of a carrot to make an extra-perfect carrot spear. She'd fawn over each cucumber, carefully pruning each cauliflower floret (always the last vegetable left on the platter), like she was angling for a Michelin star.

To me, *that* is a crudité. (Funny enough, after all that fuss, she'd just squirt a bottle of Hidden Valley ranch dressing into a bowl for the dip part.) So, unless you're carving a wooden ship out of a head of broccoli, please, don't call it a crudité. Yes, I know the word literally translates to "raw," and technically, any plate of raw vegetables can be called crudités, but I feel like that word is just so "extra." It's like, *Oh, is this a "crudité"?* A word that feels so fancy you can hardly stand it? Maybe we can leave that word out of it and simply call it a thoughtfully arranged platter of vegetables.

All that said, I am such a huge fan of setting out a thoughtfully arranged platter of vegetables to snack on when I have people over that I would be remiss not to mention it in this book. In my version, there is no theatrical carving or relentless peeling. There might be the occasional blanch or boil for things like asparagus and tiny potatoes (another reason the word *crudité* does not fly here), but more often than not, it's just a casual slice or chunk of whatever I am feeling at the moment (nearly always cucumbers, radishes of all sorts and sizes, and sweet, skinny carrots). There are certain No Fly Zone items for me, which include bell peppers (any color) and raw button mushrooms, but to each their own.

I go back and forth between wanting to season my vegetables with lemon and salt and leaving them raw, in their unadorned, natural state. If the vegetables are going to be out for a while, I won't season them (as they sit with the lemon and salt, they become weepy and wilty), but if it's a smaller crowd and I can monitor the situation, then I'll give them a squeeze of lemon and a sprinkle of salt, maybe something like sumac or crushed red pepper flakes as well. This move is good but not a necessity.

As for accompaniments, it is truly up to you. Aside from the obvious, which is that there must be at least one dip (any of the ones from pages 22–26 would be excellent), you can get as elaborate or not as you'd like (TWO dips!!). Flavored salts are also a nice touch, as are pieces of crispy ham (page 114).

Vinegar-Marinated Butter Beans

serves 4 to 8

⅓ cup olive oil
2 (15-ounce) cans butter, lima, or
   gigante beans, drained and rinsed
1 small garlic clove, finely grated
Kosher salt and freshly ground black
   pepper
½ cup red wine vinegar or white
   wine vinegar
Freshly grated lemon zest

These butter beans are just as much a snack as a side for me; I love them as part of a larger spread (perhaps with lamb, like on page 204), alongside raw vegetables (page 54), Tangy Roasted Mushrooms (page 60), and/or all the cheeses. Technically, any bean will work here, but for snacking purposes, the larger the better because trying to elegantly eat an individual cannellini bean would be nearly impossible. (On that note, they really are best eaten with toothpicks, because it's both cute and practical, two of my favorite qualifiers.)

1 Heat the olive oil in a small pot over medium heat. Add the beans and garlic and season with salt and pepper.

2 Cook a minute or two, just to warm them through and remove the I-just-came-from-a-can flavor.

3 Remove from the heat and add the vinegar, swirling to combine. Let sit at least 30 minutes.

4 Transfer the bean mixture to a small bowl or serving dish (if you want to drain them, that is okay too, but I like to serve them in their marinade) and finish with more black pepper and lemon zest.

DO AHEAD Beans can be marinated up to 2 weeks ahead, covered, and refrigerated. Bring them to room temperature before serving.

Fancy Citrusy Olives

serves 6 to 8

1 lemon

1 orange

½ cup olive oil

4 whole chiles de arbol, or
    ½ teaspoon crushed red
    pepper flakes

Peel of 1 grapefruit

1 pound unpitted Castelvetrano
    olives

NOTE *I find the unpitted olives to be of a better quality than the pitted variety, but use what you can find.*

I know, I said nothing fancy! But these olives deserve the title. Great straight from the briny bath they came from, Castelvetrano olives are delicious as is, but warming them in a bit of citrusy olive oil with some whole chiles makes them, well, better (and kind of fancy).

Like most other things in this chapter, they can be customized to your liking, so go wild! Mix your olives! Add smashed garlic or chopped rosemary! Up the citrus! The moral of the story here is that your already good olives should be gently simmered in a flavorful olive oil to warm through and mellow their briny flavor, making them truly excellent.

1 Halve and thinly slice one half of each lemon and orange, saving the other halves for juicing.

2 Warm the olive oil in a small pot over medium heat. Add the chiles, lemon and orange slices, and grapefruit peel. Let sizzle a minute or two, then add the olives.

3 Reduce the heat to the lowest possible setting and let the olives hang out here for anywhere from 10 minutes to 1 hour, stirring every so often. (If your stove's burner is one of those that never quite gets that low, then you might want to max them out around 30 minutes.)

4 Let the olives cool to room temperature in the pot and then squeeze in the lemon and orange juice from the remaining halves. Serve with citrus peels and all, making sure you have a little dish for the olive pits.

DO AHEAD Olives can be marinated up to a month in advance, covered, and refrigerated. Gently rewarm them before serving.

Tangy Roasted Mushrooms

serves 4 to 8

2 pounds fresh mushrooms, such
    as maitake, oyster, or trumpet,
    sliced, cut, or torn into large,
    bite-sized pieces
¼ cup olive oil, plus more for
    drizzling
Kosher salt and freshly ground black
    pepper
1 small white onion or shallot, thinly
    sliced into rings
¼ cup white wine vinegar
Fresh herbs, such as parsley, chives,
    or cilantro, tender leaves and
    stems, finely chopped (optional)

NOTE *This recipe also works
well with eggplant. To do this,
cut an eggplant into ½-inch-
thick slices and roast as you
would the mushrooms, cooking
until the slices are completely
tender and nicely browned,
25 to 30 minutes. Proceed with
the recipe.*

Know that these are not pickled mushrooms; rather,
they are deeply roasted mushrooms that are doused in
vinegar and left to marinate. The main difference for
me is the texture. If you've ever had a mushroom from
the giardiniera jar, you may have found that texture a bit
slimy and squeaky, but these are not those mushrooms.
These mushrooms get roasted so their mushroomy flavor
concentrates and the texture changes from soft and slimy
to firm and meaty. From there, they get covered in a mild
vinegar bath to marinate, rather than pickle. You can go
all in with one type of mushroom, sure, but I like to mix it
up for varying textures, flavors, and price points because,
damn, mushrooms can be expensive.

1 Preheat the oven to 425°F.

2 Toss the mushrooms with the olive oil in a large cast-iron
skillet, on a rimmed baking sheet, or in a large baking dish.
Season with salt and pepper, and roast, tossing occasionally (to
help steam escape and promote even cooking) till browned and
crisped, 20 to 25 minutes.

3 Remove from the oven and place in a medium bowl. Add the
onion and vinegar, tossing to coat. Let sit at least 20 minutes
before transferring to a serving bowl or plate. Drizzle with more
olive oil and finish with a handful of fresh herbs, if you like.

DO AHEAD Mushrooms can be marinated up to 5 days ahead,
covered, and refrigerated. Add the herbs just before serving,
if using.

diy
martini bar

I used to think martinis were extremely and exclusively fancy. If you have felt this way, too, you may be asking yourself, "What is this very fancy drink doing in a book that advertises advice to the contrary?" Well, I no longer think of martinis as being extremely and exclusively fancy. Isn't that great news?

There's more great news, least of which involves you getting to drink a martini in the comfort of your own home. Just like a spritz, a martini does not require any experience in cocktail making, simply the combining of two to three ingredients in a ratio even I can remember.

Since making individual 'tinis for everyone who walks through the door is not on my agenda for any evening, I like to make one giant batch, and since shaking a giant batch of martinis is absolutely out of the question, I prefer them stirred. I've mixed my giant martini (or many regular-sized martinis) in everything from a flower vase to a Chemex coffeepot to those extremely useful IKEA water carafes to a cool jug I got a flea market and swore I'd find a use for one day. (This! This is the use!)

To make sure they're as cold and diluted as possible (both essential qualities), I serve my martinis over ice, which of course is in no way customary or probably even allowed, but it's how I do it. My house, my rules! When guests arrive, offer them your selection of beverages, including a martini. When they say, "Wow, yes, I would love a martini," smile and point them in the direction of the well-curated martini bar and say "All you, baby!"

TO MAKE (for 6 to 10 people)
For a batch of classic martinis, combine 2½ cups/20 ounces **gin** (that is my preference, but use **vodka** if you like) with 2½ cups/20 ounces **dry vermouth** and 1 cup/8 ounces of **water** in a vessel large enough to hold it all. I'd say this serves 6 to 10 since sometimes it's a one-martini night and sometimes it's a three-martini night, and, well, wouldn't you rather have some leftover than not enough? (PSA: Store any leftover mix in a glass jar in the freezer; it will keep indefinitely.)

Set out the jug o' martinis next to a bowl of ice and any garnish you desire. **Martini olives** are classique (add brine to the cocktail to make it dirty), or use a **pearl onion** instead to make it a Gibson. **Lemon peels** are nice for those classy folks wanting theirs "with a twist." Things like tiny forks, cute spoons, and toothpicks are a nice touch but not necessary. (The DIY Martini Bar is why I own 83 very cute tiny forks.)

Tiny Peppers with Yuzu Kosho

serves 4 to 6

1 pound shishito peppers
2 tablespoons vegetable oil
Kosher salt and freshly ground black
  pepper
1 tablespoon yuzu kosho
Flaky sea salt
1–2 limes, halved

It may sound silly to ask you to toss peppers with a paste made from peppers, but when the peppers in question aren't necessarily spicy, don't you miss the heat, just a little? Well, I definitely do, so I'm bringing them back from whence they came: peppers on peppers, if you will. The first peppers in question are tiny little shishito, which, sure, can be spicy, but not always.

The second pepper is more of a chile and comes in the form of yuzu kosho, a Japanese chile paste made from fermented green chiles and the rind of the yuzu fruit. It's bright, salty, citrusy, spicy, and extremely flavorful, so a little goes a long way. While I wouldn't call it "super accessible" just yet, it is becoming increasingly more available at many of the larger grocery stores (or you can always buy it online).

The tiny peppers are blistered in a skillet or grilled to get them all charred and tender, after which you toss them in a large bowl with some yuzu kosho, fresh lime juice, and lots of flaky salt for a very addictive snack.

1 Toss the shishitos with the oil in a large serving or mixing bowl and season with salt and pepper.

2 Heat a large skillet over high heat until it's extremely hot. Working in batches, if needed, add the peppers and toss occasionally until tender and well charred all over, 2 to 4 minutes. (Alternatively grill the peppers over a hot grill until well charred and blistered, 2 to 4 minutes.)

3 Return the peppers to the bowl and add the yuzu kosho and a healthy pinch of flaky salt. Squeeze the lime over everything, toss to coat and evenly distribute the yuzu kosho, and serve.

Seeded Breadsticks with Parmesan

serves 6 to 10

2 cups all-purpose flour, plus more
    for the work surface
¼ cup whole wheat, rye, spelt,
    or buckwheat flour (or more
    all-purpose)
1 teaspoon active dry yeast
1 teaspoon kosher salt
⅓ cup white and/or black
    sesame seeds
¼ cup poppy seeds
1 cup finely grated parmesan,
    plus more for finishing
¾ cup warm-ish water
2 tablespoons olive oil, plus more
    for bowl
Flaky sea salt

The word "breadstick" can mean many different things to many different people, but in case there is any confusion, these are not the soft, bready Olive Garden-y breadsticks. Rather, they are the long, skinny, crunchy, snappy breadsticks. The shape may look intimidating to pull off, but I promise that you do not need to apprentice with an Italian grandmother to get these right. This dough is extremely forgiving and easy to work with; you basically look at it and it turns into a breadstick.

If you've ever turned balls of Play-Doh into thin ropes so you can coil them and make mini beehives, you can transform this dough into long, elegant breadsticks. The trick is to roll each rope to the same even thickness; otherwise, you get parts of the breadstick that bake faster than other parts, which means uneven breadstick texture (some parts thin and crisp, some parts puffier and soft—not ideal!).

For an even better, deeper flavor, I like to add a bit of an alternative flour (i.e., rye, buckwheat, spelt, or whole wheat). You'll see that even ¼ cup makes a big difference, but if you'd rather not deal with adding another ingredient, I get that; regular all-purpose flour will work just fine. The cheese, however, is a must. I'm sure you understand.

1 Whisk the flours, yeast, and kosher salt in a large bowl to combine. Add the sesame and poppy seeds and the parmesan. Make a well in the center, and drizzle in the lukewarm water, followed by the olive oil. Using a wooden spoon (or your hands), mix until no dry spots remain and the dough still feels a bit sticky, 1 to 2 minutes.

2 Transfer the dough to a well-oiled bowl and cover tightly with plastic. Let rest at room temperature until not quite but nearly doubled in size, 60 to 90 minutes, depending on the temperature of your kitchen.

3 Preheat the oven to 375°F.

4 Line two baking sheets with parchment. Turn out the dough onto a lightly floured surface and, using the palms of your hands, flatten into a rectangle roughly 8 by 4 inches. Using a pastry scraper, bench scraper, or sharp knife, cut the dough vertically into strips about ¼ inch thick (you'll get 40 to 50 strips).

5 Cover the rest of the dough with a lightly damp kitchen or paper towel while you form the breadsticks (if the dough gets dry, it will be hard to roll out). Roll each piece of dough onto an unfloured work surface (cutting board or countertop) until you've got a long, skinny breadstick-shaped piece of dough. (They will puff slightly as they rest and once they bake, so go skinnier than you think— they should be thinner than a pencil.)

6 Place each strip of dough on the baking sheets, spaced ½ inch apart (they don't spread much) until you've filled the baking sheets. Brush or drizzle the dough with some olive oil and sprinkle with flaky salt and a showering of additional parmesan.

7 Bake, rotating the sheets once, until the breadsticks are golden brown and baked through, 8 to 10 minutes (if there are some that are thinner than others and baking quicker, feel free to pluck them from the baking sheet and continue to bake those that need it).

8 Let cool slightly before serving.

DO AHEAD Breadstick dough can be made up to 2 days ahead, wrapped tightly, and refrigerated. Breadsticks can be baked up to 2 days ahead, kept on their baking sheets (so they don't break), wrapped tightly with plastic, and stored at room temperature.

Overnight Focaccia, Tonight

serves 6 to 10

1 (¼-ounce) packet instant dry yeast or 2¼ teaspoons

2 teaspoons honey

2 tablespoons olive oil, plus lots more for coating the bowl and pan

2¼ cups warm-ish water

5 cups bread flour (all-purpose flour will also do the trick here, although the dough might be slightly less elastic), plus more for the work surface

2 teaspoons kosher salt

1 small red onion, thinly sliced into rings (about ⅛ inch thick)

Flaky sea salt

I have a lot of strengths, but "planning ahead" is absolutely not one of them. The idea that I'd make a bread dough and leave it to proof overnight so that it can develop flavor and structure to bake the next evening is a really great idea, and something that I have done before. But a more likely scenario is that around 3 p.m. the day I'm planning on having people over, I think *Wouldn't it be nice to have fresh focaccia with dinner tonight?* Yes, it would be!

And so, because I am the master of my own destiny, I spent some time cheating the system and disgracing professional bakers everywhere, developing a focaccia that can be made in just a few hours. Does it use freshly milled grains and a naturally fermented 58-year-old starter? No. Is it fluffy and light and oily and crispy and tender and chewy? Absolutely. If you *do* have the time, it will of course benefit from an overnight rest in the refrigerator, but if you *don't* have the time, just know that you will still have something truly excellent.

I like this focaccia on the simple side, with a ridiculous amount of olive oil, lots of flaky salt, and thin slices of red onion that get all caramelized and crisped, but you could absolutely get creative, topping it with chopped herbs, chopped garlic, a sprinkle of sesame seeds, anchovies (!!), thin slices of ripe tomato . . . the list goes on. Just know that there is a fine line between focaccia and pizza, so don't overdo it with the topping (unless, of course, you're looking for pizza, in which case, check out page 266).

1 Whisk the yeast, honey, 2 tablespoons olive oil, and water in a large bowl. Add the flour and, using a wooden spoon, mix to casually blend (it will still be a craggy mess; that's fine). Add the kosher salt and continue to mix until it goes from craggy to kind of wet and shaggy (the dough is going to be too wet and sticky to knead at this stage, so don't worry about getting it nice and smooth yet). Cover tightly with plastic wrap and let sit in a warm spot until it doubles in size, about an hour or so.

2 Turn the dough out onto a lightly floured surface and, using the palm of one hand, press into the dough, turning and folding it onto itself (a.k.a. kneading) a few times (the dough will still be sticky but much more manageable) until it comes together and starts looking smooth and elastic. Feel free to dust with flour occasionally but not too much.

3 Once the dough is looking nice and smooth, drizzle a bit of olive oil into that same bowl to grease it up and put dough back. Cover the bowl tightly with plastic wrap and let sit in a warm spot until it doubles in size again, another 45 to 60 minutes.

4 Pour enough olive oil onto a rimmed baking sheet (approximately 12¾ by 17¾ inches) to generously coat the entire sheet. Using your hands, spread it all around. Turn the dough onto the baking sheet and again using your hands, coax the dough into a flat, even layer. (It doesn't need to stretch to the exact size of the sheet pan; it'll puff up and fill in as it proofs and bakes.) Drizzle the top with lots more olive oil and lightly drape a piece of plastic over for its final nap, letting it rest in a warm spot for another 45 to 60 minutes.

5 Preheat the oven to 425°F.

6 To know when the dough is ready to bake, it should look light, puffy, and buoyant. To test this, use your fingertips to press the dough lightly. It should bounce back ever so slightly. (If it sinks and deflates, well, you've overproofed the dough and it might never recover. But let's not assume the worst. Even then, you'll still have something edible; just call it flatbread.) Using the tips of your fingers to lightly dimple the surface, kind of like you're playing the piano, scatter the top with the onion rings and drizzle again with, yes, more olive oil, and sprinkle with flaky salt. Bake, rotating if needed to avoid hot spots, until the bread is deeply golden brown and the onion rings are caramelized and cooked through, 35 to 45 minutes.

7 Remove from the oven and let cool slightly before slicing and serving.

DO AHEAD The dough can be made 1 day ahead. Just wrap tightly after step 3 and refrigerate.

A Better Garlic Bread / Caramelized Garlic on Toast with Anchovies

serves 4 to 8

1 head of garlic, cloves separated, peeled, and smashed with the back of a knife

½ cup olive oil

1 (2-ounce) tin anchovies (or half of a 4-ounce jar), drained

½ cup (1 stick) unsalted butter, softened

Pinch of crushed red pepper flakes (optional)

Kosher salt and freshly ground black pepper

1 or 2 baguettes, halved lengthwise

Flaky sea salt

Finely chopped fresh parsley (optional)

NOTE *This butter mixture makes enough for 1 or 2 baguettes, depending on the baguette, but start with one and either way you'll have some leftover—because to run out of garlic butter would be a true crime.*

Garlic bread is one of life's finest, simplest pleasures, up there with a roast chicken and a perfect salad with lemon. It's basic and should not be overthought. But do not treat it or mistake this as garlic butter on toast—or worse, soggy bread soaked in garlic butter—garlic bread is neither.

The secret is treating it like french toast in the sense that you really, truly do need to soak the hell out of it, ensuring that the edges get golden brown and crisped while the center stays soft and tender.

Yes, the anchovies are a secret weapon, but the garlic cloves, slowly softening and caramelizing in the oil, are the real hero. Don't worry about getting the cloves too broken up—a few pieces here and there are a welcome addition.

1 Preheat the oven to 425°F.

2 Heat the garlic and oil in a small pot over medium heat. Cook until the garlic has started to audibly sizzle, about 3 minutes. Reduce the heat to the lowest possible setting and continue to cook until the garlic is totally tender and golden brown, 15 to 20 minutes. Add the anchovies and remove from heat.

3 Transfer the oil mixture to a medium bowl along with the butter and red pepper flakes. Using a fork, smash everything together so that the garlic cloves break down and everything turns into a delicious, creamy paste. Season with salt and pepper. Using a spoon, evenly distribute this deliciousness onto each half of the bread, letting it really soak in there.

4 Place the bread on a rimmed baking sheet and bake until the edges are golden brown, with soft and supple centers (the only time I'll use the word *supple*), 8 to 10 minutes. Remove from oven and sprinkle with flaky salt and parsley, if using.

DO AHEAD Garlic butter can be made 1 week ahead, wrapped tightly, and stored in the refrigerator. Bring to room temperature before smearing onto the bread.

Spicy, Giant Crunchy Corn

serves 6 to 8

4 cups large corn nuts ("quicos")

3 tablespoons vegetable oil

Kosher salt and freshly ground black pepper

2 tablespoons Aleppo-style pepper or Korean pepper flakes

⅓ cup nutritional yeast

Popcorn is one of my all-time favorite snacks, but I file it under the "personal snack" category, as in, "I am not going to eat popcorn in front of other people." It's a real mess, every time, which is fine when you're alone on the couch or in a very dark movie theater, where nobody can witness you shoveling tiny kernels of popped corn into your mouth, missing a few every time, crumbs absolutely everywhere. But in front of company? I would never.

That said, I do think that the larger corn nuts, a.k.a. "quicos," are a great approximation with at least 85 percent less mess, and you can dress them up however you want. While they come already oiled and salted, I enjoy gussying them up even further and treating them like I treat my popcorn—with lots of nutritional yeast, Aleppo-style pepper, and more salt. They are wildly addictive and will probably upstage anything else you serve, so be prepared.

1 Preheat the oven to 325°F.

2 On a rimmed baking sheet, toss the corn nuts with the oil and season with the salt and pepper. Roast, tossing occasionally, until corn is smelling toasted and is a deeper shade of golden brown, 10 to 12 minutes.

3 Remove from the oven and immediately transfer the corn nuts to a large bowl. Add the Aleppo-style pepper and nutritional yeast, and toss to coat.

DO AHEAD Crunchy corn can be made up to 5 days ahead, stored in a tight-fitting plastic container or glass jar.

Slightly Sticky Walnuts with Sesame and Sumac

serves 6

4 cups raw walnuts pieces
(about 12 ounces)
⅓ cup pure maple syrup
¼ cup tahini
¼ cup raw white sesame seeds
2 tablespoons olive oil
Pinch of cayenne or crushed red
pepper flakes
Kosher salt and freshly ground black
pepper
1 tablespoon ground sumac
Flaky sea salt, such as Maldon

NOTE *I buy walnut "pieces" because not only do they save you a step, but they are also less expensive. If using whole, just lightly crush them before proceeding with the recipe.*

These slightly sticky walnuts are better than anything you can find in the bulk bins at Whole Foods, I promise. Not as sweet as you'd think, given all that maple syrup (which coats the nuts as they roast, leaving you with some deliciously mapley, crystallized sugar), they also happen to be extra nutty thanks to tahini and a sprinkling of sesame seeds. As if that weren't exciting enough, they're also tangy from the sumac and delightfully salty from flaky salt. Kind of the perfect one-stop-shop, highly addictive, very snackable nut.

I will also mention that they are extremely low maintenance and easy to make. Basically, you toss a bunch of stuff together on a baking sheet and bake. No stovetop stirring, no candy thermometers, no fussiness. Nothing fancy!

You can definitely mix up the nuts here (pecans would be nice), but walnuts are always the first to go, so why not cut to the chase and give the people what they want?

1 Preheat the oven to 325°F. Line a rimmed baking sheet with parchment, or use a large oven-safe skillet and don't worry about the parchment.

2 Place the walnuts on the baking sheet and drizzle the maple syrup over, followed by the tahini, sesame seeds, olive oil, and cayenne. Season with salt and pepper, and toss to combine so that everything is evenly coated.

3 Roast, stirring occasionally, until the walnuts are golden brown and the maple syrup is caramelized, 15 to 20 minutes.

4 Remove from heat and immediately sprinkle with the sumac and flaky salt, tossing to coat. Let cool completely before serving.

DO AHEAD These walnuts can be made up to 5 days ahead, stored in a tight glass jar or plastic container. If it's humid outside and they feel sticky at all, just reheat them in a 325°F oven for a few minutes to dry out a bit.

salad bar croutons

Every now and then I have a moment when something I eat blows me away, either by its ingenuity or its deliciousness or sometimes both. Sitting down to what is probably still one of the best lunches of my life at a small restaurant in Sicily, I was served a bowl of croutons as a snack, presumably made from yesterday's bread. Reader, I was *blown away!* I know, a crouton in general, is fine, but croutons as a snack? Without salad? Without a roasted chicken? Just a bowl of highly seasoned, herby croutons to nibble on while you wait for more bowls of croutons? *It was the most brilliant thing I have ever seen.* So, while I'd love to take credit, I simply cannot. I can only pass along the genius to you.

TO MAKE

Nearly any loaf of bread will do, but know that these croutons are extremely good made with leftover **focaccia** (page 70). Cut or tear your bread of choice into bite-sized pieces. Toss on a rimmed baking sheet with a clove or two of finely chopped **garlic** if you like garlicky things and/or a pinch of **red pepper** flakes if you like spicy things. Add enough **olive oil** to soak them pretty well (they should be pretty oily), then season with salt and pepper.

   Bake in a 425°F oven, tossing occasionally, until they're crispy and golden brown on the outside, but still kind of tender and chewy on the inside, 10 to 15 minutes (they will firm as they cool, so good to test one on the counter when you think they might be done). Remove from the oven, and let cool before snacking on or adding to your salad.

   For an Italian-Seasoning-Croutons-Out-of-a-Bag vibe, keep the **garlic** and **chili flakes** and add **finely chopped fresh herbs** like **thyme, rosemary, oregano,** or **marjoram** and a good sprinkle of **dried onion** or **garlic powder** before baking.

   For Sumac Croutons, keep the **garlic** and add about 1 tablespoon of **dried sumac** before baking.

salads

These days, a salad can be anything you want it to be.

But here, I am focusing on what traditionally defines the genre: a cold or ambient-temperature, mostly vegetable—sometimes fruit—based dish, typically composed of crunchy produce, leafy greens, or a combination of both. Salads are not-so-secretly my favorite chapter, since they exist on the table to provide freshness, texture, and acidity—my three favorite things. I have categorized salads into what I believe are the most important types: Leafy, Crunchy, and Kind-of Salads. While all different, they share my universal salad truths:

No vinaigrettes. Not only do you not need two bowls for what you can do in one, but salads are to be dressed and seasoned like all other food—first with salt and acid (citrus or vinegar) until it's salty and acidic enough, and *then* with fat (olive oil, probably) to round out all the flavors.

On that note, **salads must be hyper acidic and pleasingly salty.** I'm talking to the point where each bite is as addictive as a bag of Cool Ranch Doritos.

No creamy dressings. This is an aesthetic choice as much as it is a taste preference. If a particular salad needs something rich and creamy, I prefer to treat that rich and creamy something more like a dip, spooned under the other ingredients for swiping and dragging.

Just like when a sandwich tastes better if cut into triangles, **salads taste better when eaten from a shallow bowl or plate.** I don't make the rules; I only enforce them.

Escarole with Mustard and Spicy Guanciale Bread Crumbs

serves 4 to 6

1 shallot, thinly sliced into rings

2 tablespoons red wine vinegar or white wine vinegar

Kosher salt and freshly ground black pepper

3 ounces guanciale or pancetta, cut into ½-inch pieces

¾ cup fresh bread crumbs (see page 14) or panko

½ teaspoon crushed red pepper flakes, plus more for seasoning

1 garlic clove, finely grated

1 large head of escarole, torn into large pieces

1 cup fresh parsley, tender leaves and stems

3 tablespoons whole-grain mustard

3 tablespoons olive oil

¼ cup nutritional yeast (optional)

NOTE *The "nutritional yeast as cheese" is something I learned from my friend/chef/ excellent dancer Gerardo Gonzalez. It's sprinkled over his famous-to-me vegan Caesar, at one of my favorite NYC pizza spots, Scarr's. The nutty, umami-y nutritional yeast acts as a lighter, brighter parmesan.*

Sort of a gateway chicory, escarole is on the mild end of the spectrum as far as bitterness goes, but like everything in the chicory family, it's still best dressed and eaten with fatty things to mitigate some of that bitterness.

Luckily, this salad has plenty of fatty things—specifically, guanciale, which is like a porkier, more delicately seasoned pancetta. Unlike pancetta, guanciale is nearly all fat, but rather than dissolve in a hot skillet like you might expect, it crisps as it renders, leaving you with both tiny crispy bits to nibble on and a glorious, shiny pool of pork fat for which to toast bread crumbs in. The very best of every world.

1 Combine the shallot and vinegar in a small bowl and season with salt and pepper; let sit a few minutes.

2 Heat the guanciale in a large skillet over medium-low heat. Cook, stirring occasionally, until guanciale has rendered most of the fat and is starting to brown and crisp, 10 to 12 minutes (do not try to do this faster, or it will brown and crisp before fat is rendered, and fat is what we are after).

3 Add the bread crumbs and crushed red pepper flakes to the skillet. Season with salt and pepper and continue to cook until the bread crumbs are nicely golden brown and toasted, 3 to 4 minutes. Remove from the heat and add the garlic, stirring to mix in.

4 Toss the escarole, parsley, mustard, and shallot with the vinegar in a large bowl. Season with salt and pepper and add the olive oil. Give it another toss and transfer to a large serving platter. Top with the nutritional yeast (if using) and some of the bread crumbs, serving any extra alongside.

DO AHEAD Bread crumbs can be made up to 2 days ahead, tightly covered, and refrigerated. Gently rewarm before serving.

Chicories with Preserved Lemon, Yogurt, and Mint

serves 4 to 6

1 cup full-fat Greek yogurt

4 tablespoons fresh lemon juice, divided, plus more as needed

Kosher salt and freshly ground black pepper

½ preserved lemon, seeds removed, thinly sliced into strips

½ garlic clove, finely grated

2 heads of radicchio, Castelfranco, treviso, or other variety of chicory, torn or sliced into 2-inch pieces

1 cup fresh mint leaves, plus more for serving

¼ cup olive oil, plus more for serving

4 to 6 anchovy fillets, drained (optional)

EAT WITH
Hard-Roasted Spiced Cauliflower (page 150)
+
Yogurt-Marinated Leg of Lamb with Spicy Fennel and Sumac (page 204)

This is not like a casual "I'll just have a bowl of this salad for lunch" type of salad. This bitter, sassy, garlicky salad needs and wants a friend. A rich, hearty friend like leg of lamb (page 204) or spicy pork shoulder (page 209). Not that the fattiness of the yogurt or freshness of mint leaves don't adequately tame the bitterness of the chicories; they do, but it's still the kind of vegetable that needs other things on the table.

For whatever reason, I am just not a fan of coating each leaf individually with a creamy dressing (yes, I am a "dressing on the side" person) and I prefer to drag and dip my perky, seasoned lettuces through a tangy sauce rather than weigh down the leaves with a dressing, making them all sad and wilty. However, this is a no-judgment zone and if you *are* into salads fully tossed with creamy dressings, you can absolutely thin this yogurt number down with enough water as needed and use it as such, drizzling over the chicories and tossing to coat before serving.

1 Whisk the yogurt and 2 tablespoons lemon juice together in a small bowl; season with salt and pepper. It should be pleasantly tangy and salty; season with more lemon juice and salt, if needed.

2 Combine the preserved lemon, garlic, and remaining 2 tablespoons lemon juice in a large bowl. Add the chicories, mint, and olive oil and toss to coat. Season with salt and plenty of pepper.

3 Smear the yogurt mixture onto the bottom of a large serving bowl or plate and top with the salad.

4 Drizzle with more olive oil as desired, and scatter additional mint and the anchovies, if using, over the top before serving.

DO AHEAD Yogurt sauce can be made up to 3 days ahead, covered, and refrigerated. The greens can be prepped and torn and tossed with mint a day ahead, stored in a zippered bag, and refrigerated.

perfect herby salad

How many times in your life have you said, "Wow, this is a perfect salad!"? I say it all the time because I am prone to hyperbole, but when I do say it, it's because I'm eating a bowl of very fresh and spicy greens dressed with herbs, lemon, olive oil, and flaky sea salt. To me, this salad is perfect, and yes that is a *Love, Actually* reference.

Not to fluff my own feathers, but every time I serve this perfect salad, people freak out. "WHAT is in this salad? WHAT did you put on it??? IT IS SO GOOD!" And I get it! How is it possible that simple greens, tossed with leafy herbs, squeezed with a little lemon, sprinkled with a little flaky salt, and drizzled with a little olive oil could be so life-changingly good?

The caveat here is that it requires a bit of "extra work" on your part, and by "extra work," I mean "visit a farmers' market." All fruits and vegetables start to lose water the minute they are picked from wherever they come from (The dirt! A tree! A bush!), but none more apparently or rapidly than lettuce or salad greens. This means the greens procured from a farmers' market are going to be fresher, perkier, and crunchier with tons more flavor than anything that's been sitting on a supermarket shelf. When I was nineteen, I worked for a farm called Maggie's Farm located at the Wednesday/Saturday Santa Monica Farmers' Market. They paid me half in real American dollars and half in a spicy salad mix, which I never got sick of snacking on like chips during my drive home in Los Angeles traffic. Unfortunately, those greens spoiled me for life.

TO MAKE

For 4 to 6 people, start with either 6 to 8 cups **pre-mixed greens** (farmers' markets always have the best mesclun mixes) or simply a few perfect heads of neon-green **Little Gems**, baby **red leaf**, tiny **romaine**, or tight little roses of **butter lettuce**, leaves pulled apart and torn if large. Then, mix in **a LOT of fresh herbs** (tender leaves AND stems, of course) like **parsley, chives, dill, mint, tarragon, or cilantro** (whatever mix turns you on, go for it). The ratio should almost be 50/50.

To dress this very special and simple salad, I skip the vinaigrette altogether (which, if you've read any of these other salad recipes, you'll notice is a theme). Simply squeeze half a **lemon** over, tossing to make sure every leaf is nicely coated, but not wet or soggy. Sprinkle with some **flaky salt** and a good grind of **black pepper**. Taste a leaf or two; does it need more lemon? Squeeze some more over. More salt? Give it another sprinkle. Each leaf should taste like a pleasantly lemony, salty version of itself (green, fresh, lettuce-y, spicy if applicable). Drizzle with a bit of **good olive oil** and toss just to coat—not too much or the leaves could become heavy.

You can serve this salad with literally anything on the planet, or use it as a bed for a nicely poached egg and whatever leftovers you've got swimming about in your fridge for a better version of whatever fast-casual salad bar you're obsessed with at the moment. To me, it is perfect—I think you'll think so, too.

Lemony Watercress with Raw and Toasted Fennel

serves 4 to 6

1 tablespoon fennel seeds

1 Meyer or regular lemon, thinly
  sliced, seeds removed

2 tablespoons fresh lemon juice

1 small shallot, thinly sliced or finely
  chopped

Kosher salt and freshly ground black
  pepper

1 bunch watercress, arugula, or baby
  mustard greens, thick stem ends
  trimmed

1 fennel bulb, thinly sliced

Olive oil, for drizzling

NOTE *The hydroponic
watercress tends to be
painfully delicate, wispy, and
almost anemic in flavor, fine
for things like garnishes, but I
wouldn't recommend using it
in salads like this. If you can't
find the heartier stuff, use
something like good arugula
or baby mustard greens.*

Not all watercress is created equal. There's the wild stuff, the cultivated stuff, and the hydroponic stuff. Wild, it grows like a weed wherever there is good, fresh, gently running water, near creeks, brooks, and slow-moving rivers (hence the name, "watercress"). This is the king of all watercresses, hearty and spicy, spriggy and leafy, and insanely flavorful. It's available seasonally at farmers' markets and specialty grocery stores in both purple (!!) and deep army green. I wouldn't call it an easily found ingredient, but the cultivated stuff is a good approximation.

Mostly a salad to celebrate the specialness of a good, peppery watercress, there is also crunchy fennel tossed with some thin (whole) lemon slices. I enjoy the assertive acidity and gentle bitterness of the whole lemon, which, coupled with the spiciness of the greens, makes this kind of an "adult salad," which is, incidentally, my new favorite phrase. Serve it with anything that has more subtle, quiet flavors, like the Chicken and Mushroom Skillet Pie (page 200) or the Grilled Trout with Green Goddess Butter (page 244).

1 Toast the fennel seeds in a small skillet over medium heat, shaking constantly until they are smelling super fragrant and are a light golden brown, about 1 minute.

2 Add the seeds to a small bowl along with the lemon slices, lemon juice, and shallot; season with salt and pepper. Let sit a few minutes just to slightly soften the lemon.

3 Combine the watercress and fennel in a large bowl. Add the lemon mixture and toss to combine. Season with salt and pepper and drizzle with olive oil before serving.

DO AHEAD The watercress and fennel can be tossed together a day ahead, stored in a zippered bag, and refrigerated. Dress with the lemon mixture just before serving.

Little Gems with Garlicky Lemon and Pistachio

serves 4 to 6

2 lemons

½ cup raw pistachios, almonds, or walnuts, finely chopped

1 garlic clove, finely grated

¼ cup olive oil, plus more for drizzling

Kosher salt and freshly ground black pepper

4–6 heads of Little Gem lettuce (1½–2 pounds) or 1 large head of romaine or iceberg, quartered

½ cup fresh parsley, tender leaves and stems, coarsely chopped

½ cup fresh chopped chives

¼ cup fresh dill, coarsely chopped

Flaky sea salt

This is the salad of my dreams. Garlicky, bracingly acidic, clean, and crunchy as hell. The denim jacket of salads, it complements just about everything. Dress it up or dress it down, eat it alone or with 24 other things. To say anything else about this salad would be doing it a disservice, because every minute reading another word about it is a minute you're not going to the store to get ingredients for this salad to make immediately.

Little Gem lettuces may seem like a myth, but they do exist and you can find them. If you can't, a head of romaine, or even my best friend, iceberg lettuce, will do the trick; the point is that you should seek out a lettuce with adequate sturdiness and abundant crunch. Similarly, if pistachios aren't your thing, you can use most any other nut, including but not limited to almonds or walnuts.

1 Finely chop one of the lemons, taking care to avoid and remove all seeds. Zest and juice the remaining lemon; set aside.

2 Toast the pistachios in a small skillet over medium heat until they're just starting to smell toasty but before they turn brown, 2 to 3 minutes. Remove from the heat and place in a medium bowl; let cool.

3 Add the lemon zest, chopped lemon, garlic, and olive oil to the pistachios and season with salt and pepper.

4 Scatter the Little Gems onto a large serving platter or shallow bowl. Drizzle with the lemon juice and a bit of olive oil until all the bits get some love; season with salt and pepper.

5 Spoon the pistachio mixture over, followed by the herbs and flaky salt.

DO AHEAD Pistachio mixture sans garlic and whole lemon can be made a day ahead. (Lemon can get bitter as it sits, so I prefer to add it just before using.)

Iceberg with Pecorino, Crushed Olives, and Pickled Chile

serves 4 to 6

1 fresh chile, such as jalapeño, Fresno, or habanero, thinly sliced, seeds removed for less heat

½ small white or yellow onion, thinly sliced

¼ cup distilled white vinegar or white wine vinegar

2 teaspoons honey

Kosher salt and freshly ground black pepper

8 ounces Castelvetrano or oil-cured black olives, pitted and crushed

3 tablespoons fresh oregano, coarsely chopped, or 2 teaspoons dried, plus more for serving

1 head of iceberg lettuce, cut into 1½-inch wedges and leaves pulled apart slightly

½ cup fresh parsley, tender leaves and stems

6 tablespoons olive oil

1 ounce pecorino cheese, finely grated (about ½ cup), plus more, if you like

EAT WITH
Lamb Chops for the Table (page 229)
+
A Very Good Lasagna (page 256)

Iceberg lettuce, historically speaking, has a reputation for being boring, basic, and just generally uncool. But like Birkenstocks and Tevas, what was once so uncool is now the coolest. And just like Birkenstocks, I now own at least one pair of iceberg lettuce. What I'm trying to say is that I'm proud to declare that I don't just tolerate iceberg, I love iceberg. I want it. I crave it. I shop specifically for it.

Presumably named either for the watery flavor, extremely crunchy texture, or both, iceberg's name and lackluster visual appearance don't do much to sell itself, and it's sure not known for its nutritional value, but that's not why we are here. Undeniably the crunchiest in the lettuce kingdom, iceberg's neutral flavor supports being blanketed with too much cheese and scattered with salty, assertively flavored olives. If you play your cards right (and we are playing our cards very right), iceberg can be the most over-the-top, indulgent—dare I say coolest—vegetable out there (and, no, that is not an iceberg pun, but it could be!).

1 Combine the chile, onion, vinegar, and honey in a large bowl; season with salt and pepper and set aside for 5 or so minutes to soften and marinate the onion.

2 Add the olives and oregano to the onion and toss to coat.

3 Arrange the lettuce and parsley on a large serving platter or in a bowl. Spoon the onion-olive mixture over. Season with salt and pepper and drizzle with olive oil. Scatter with the cheese and more oregano, if desired, before serving.

DO AHEAD This is kind of an *à la minute* salad, but if you must, you can cut the iceberg lettuce a few hours ahead, and store it in a zippered bag in the refrigerator.

Salted Citrus Salad
with Fennel, Radish, and Olive

serves 4 to 6

¼ cup Castelvetrano or oil-cured black olives, pitted and crushed

¼ cup olive oil

4 tangerines or 2 oranges or 2 blood oranges (or some combination), peeled and sliced into ¼-inch rounds, seeds removed

Kosher salt and freshly ground black pepper

Honey, as needed

2 tablespoons fresh lemon or lime juice, plus more as needed

1 fennel bulb, trimmed and thinly sliced lengthwise

1 small or ½ large watermelon radish, very thinly sliced (or 4 regular radishes, thinly sliced)

EAT WITH
Lemony White Beans and Escarole with Anchovy and Parmesan (page 175)
+
Simple roasted chicken

Everyone needs a good citrus salad in their life, and this is a very good one. Sure, citrus is soft and I would definitely call this a "Crunchy Salad." But don't worry; there is plenty of fennel and radish to make up for any softness going on, I assure you. Since we don't all live in a place where there is access to flawless citrus year-round (good for *you*, California!), you must act and react to whatever you've got. Until you, too, move west, there is no shame in correcting the balance of tart and sweet in your bodega citrus with things like honey and additional juice from lemons or limes!

1 Combine the olives and olive oil; set aside.

2 Place the citrus on a large serving plate or platter. Season with salt, pepper, and then a little honey or lemon juice as needed to make sure everything is tasting as sweet, sour, and balanced as possible.

3 Toss the fennel, radish and 2 tablespoons lemon juice in a medium bowl; season with salt and pepper, adding more lemon juice and salt as needed to make them very tangy and almost too salty.

4 Top the citrus with the fennel-radish mixture and spoon the olive mixture over all of that. Finish with lots of black pepper.

DO AHEAD Citrus can be peeled and sliced a few hours ahead, wrapped, and refrigerated. Fennel and radish can be sliced a few hours ahead, covered, and refrigerated.

Celery and Fennel with Walnuts and Blue Cheese

serves 4 to 6

½ cup toasted walnuts (see page 14), coarsely chopped

Kosher salt and freshly ground black pepper

4 celery stalks, with leaves, thinly sliced on the bias

1 large fennel bulb, trimmed and thinly sliced lengthwise

½ small shallot, thinly sliced

2 tablespoons fresh lemon juice, plus more as needed

¼ cup olive oil, plus more as needed and for drizzling

1½ ounces firm blue cheese, such as Bayley Hazen or Valdeon, or a mild Stilton, thinly sliced or crumbled

Unfortunately for celery, the nicest thing most people can say about it is that they like to eat it with their buffalo wings; but the merits of this very good and underrated vegetable are plenty, and well . . . I LOVE CELERY. Aside from its extremely crunchy texture, gorgeous neon-green color, and crisp, green flavor, it is cheap as hell. I would be very happy with a salad made from just thinly sliced celery, lots of lemon, salt, and pepper (I would!), but nobody is going to win *Supermarket Sweep* by purchasing those ingredients alone. (In case you don't know, *Supermarket Sweep* is a now obsolete, truly absurd game show on which people win by spending the most money possible at the grocery store. Please do yourself a favor next time you have five minutes to kill and watch YouTube clips of this show.)

The point is that you can go a little bit high-low here and maybe dress up that frugal celery with some admittedly less frugal walnuts and a fancy blue cheese, and it still won't break the bank. This salad, with equal parts clean and crisp/rich and creamy, is ideal for pairing with a simple roasted chicken (or one dusted with fennel seed, like on page 189), a pot of spicy short ribs (page 224), and maybe a bowl of herby grains (page 164) or vinegared potatoes (page 163).

1 Toss the walnuts with a bit of olive oil so they are nicely coated, then season with salt and pepper and set aside.

2 Toss the celery stalks (reserve the leaves for garnish), fennel, shallot, and lemon juice in a large bowl; season with salt and pepper. Drizzle with the olive oil and season with enough lemon juice to make it very tangy.

3 Transfer to a large serving platter or large shallow bowl and top with the walnuts, cheese, celery leaves, and another drizzle of olive oil and plenty of pepper.

Citrusy Cucumbers with Red Onion and Toasted Sesame

serves 4 to 6

½ small red onion, thinly sliced
3 tablespoons tahini
1 tablespoon toasted sesame oil
3 tablespoons water
Kosher salt and freshly ground black
    pepper
1 hothouse or 4 Persian cucumbers,
    thinly sliced into rounds
2 tablespoons fresh lemon or
    lime juice
1 tablespoon finely grated lemon or
    lime zest
½ teaspoon ground sumac, plus
    more as needed (optional)
½ cup fresh cilantro, tender leaves
    and stems
3 tablespoons white or black sesame
    seeds, toasted
Olive oil, for drizzling

I love cucumbers, maybe even more than I love celery (which is saying a lot). I always have at least half a hothouse or a few Persian cucumbers in my fridge, ready to be turned into a snack or a salad like this one, where they can truly shine. (I am a true cucumber purist so don't love them in leafy salads.) Since they've got such a clean, neutral flavor, they get along with nearly all ingredients, but especially the creamy, fatty ones like tahini, yogurt, or cheese. Sorry to get you excited, but there is no cheese in this recipe. There is, however, a deeply sesame-y, creamy yet dairy-free tahini sauce that I think just might make you forget cheese exists altogether (at least for a few minutes).

This is the kind of dish that can be served as part of a "snacks for dinner" spread, but also as a salad alongside things like Swordfish with Crushed Olives and Oregano (page 243) or One-Pot Chicken with Dates and Caramelized Lemon (page 194).

1 Place the onion in a bowl of ice water and let sit 5 to 10 minutes to take the edge off; drain.

2 Whisk the tahini, sesame oil, and water in a small bowl until smooth and creamy, adding a splash of water as needed. Season with salt and pepper and set aside.

3 Toss the cucumbers, onion, lemon juice, lemon zest, and sumac (if using) together in a medium bowl; season with salt and pepper.

4 Spoon the tahini sauce onto the bottom of a large serving plate and top with the cucumbers, cilantro, sesame seeds, a drizzle of olive oil, and more sumac, if you like.

DO AHEAD Tahini sauce can be made up to 5 days ahead, stored in a container, and refrigerated.

Spicy Red Cabbage with Sweet Onion and Lime

serves 4 to 6

1 jalapeño or fresh red chile,
  finely grated or chopped

⅓ cup fresh lime juice, plus more
  for seasoning

1 tablespoon mild honey, such as
  orange blossom

1 teaspoon crushed red pepper
  flakes, plus more for seasoning

2 teaspoons ground sumac, plus
  more for seasoning

2 small heads (or 1 large head) of
  red cabbage, cores removed, very
  thinly sliced

1 red or sweet yellow onion, thinly
  sliced

Kosher salt and freshly ground black
  pepper

Olive oil, for drizzling

EAT WITH

Crushed Baby Potatoes with Scallion,
Celery, and Lots of Dill (page 135)
+
Sausage Party (page 184)

I know this will make a lot of eyes roll, but I hate the word *slaw*. Worse, *coleslaw*. I don't want to "yuck anyone's yum," but this is my book and if I decide not to call something a slaw, even though anyone could see that clearly it is, that's my prerogative. So, here we have a spicy red cabbage SALAD, which is exactly the kind of crunchy, lime-y, spicy thing that you crave when eating anything that feels kind of heavy, like stewed, braised, or grilled meats. It can also be served as sort of a bonus salad, since it takes about 3 seconds to throw together using ingredients you can easily and affordably procure.

Feel free to mix this up, using green cabbage instead of red, adding an apple if you like things on the sweeter side. It should be tangy and crunchy, and taste just how you want, so if a shredded carrot is what you want, go for it. It should also be mentioned that while, yes, it will soften slightly, this salad keeps for days in the fridge, lightly pickling and getting better with age—just like all of us.

1 Combine the jalapeño, lime juice, honey, crushed red pepper flakes, and sumac in a large bowl. Add the cabbage and onion and season with salt and pepper; let sit a few minutes.

2 Toss again to coat and season again with salt, pepper, and more crushed red pepper flakes, sumac, and lime juice, if you like. Drizzle with olive oil just before serving.

DO AHEAD Cabbage can be sliced up to 2 days ahead, kept in a zippered plastic bag or otherwise covered tightly, and stored in the refrigerator. Salad can be made 3 days ahead.

Celery Salad with Cilantro and Sesame

serves 4 to 6

2 tablespoons white sesame seeds

6 scallions, green and white parts, thinly sliced on the bias

4 celery stalks and leaves, very thinly sliced on the bias

1 bunch fresh cilantro, tender leaves and stems, cut into 2-inch pieces

1 fresh green chile, such as Thai, jalapeño, or Bird's Eye, seeds removed, thinly sliced

1 tablespoon fish sauce

3 tablespoons unseasoned rice wine vinegar, plus more as needed

2 tablespoons fresh lime juice, plus more as needed

Kosher salt and freshly ground black pepper

2 tablespoons canola oil

1 tablespoon toasted sesame oil

¼ cup olive oil, plus more for drizzling

My humble homage to New York City, this salad is inspired by a restaurant I probably eat at more than any other place: X'ian Famous Foods. It's a western Chinese-style spot with several locations around New York City, which means when a craving strikes, no matter where you are in Queens, Brooklyn, or Manhattan, you can treat yourself. And I do treat myself. Often. Anyway. I don't know exactly what's in their version of this salad; all I know is that it's 80 percent cilantro stems and 15 percent celery, and 5 percent other stuff like scallions and sesame oil. It's the perfect thing to eat when getting down on intensely lamb-y noodles or crazy-hot dumplings, but since I started making my own version (I added fish sauce and lime juice, and there's a heavier ratio of celery to other stuff), I realized I liked eating it with just about everything, but especially things like hot-and-sour chicken (page 196) or soy-braised brisket (page 226).

Honestly, though, sometimes I'll just make one to eat by itself because I am truly "Wild About Celery" (the title of my forthcoming memoir), especially in the summer when it's too hot outside to eat anything but a bowl of salty, tangy, herby celery.

1 Toast the sesame seeds in a small skillet over medium-high heat until golden brown and starting to pop, about 2 minutes. Remove from the heat and set aside.

2 Toss the scallions, celery, cilantro, chile, fish sauce, vinegar, and lime juice together in a large bowl. Season with salt and pepper and add the oils. Season again with more salt and pepper, adding more lime juice or vinegar if you like.

3 Transfer to a large bowl or serving platter and top with the sesame seeds, lots of pepper, and a drizzle of olive oil.

DO AHEAD Scallions, celery, cilantro, and chile can be combined a day ahead, stored in a large zippered bag, and refrigerated. Dress before serving.

Vinegared Apples with Persimmon and White Cheddar

serves 4 to 6

2 large, firm, tart apples, such as
    Pink Lady, Honeycrisp, or Gold
    Rush, cored and thinly sliced
2 Fuyu persimmons or Asian pears,
    thinly sliced
2 tablespoons apple cider vinegar or
    white wine vinegar, plus more for
    seasoning
2 teaspoons honey, plus more for
    seasoning
Flaky sea salt
Coarsely ground black pepper
1 knob of fresh horseradish, for
    grating, or 1 teaspoon prepared
    horseradish
1½–2 ounces sharp white cheddar
    or Gouda
Olive oil, for drizzling

EAT WITH
Garlicky Broccoli and Greens with
Hazelnut and Coriander (page 160)
+
Harissa-Rubbed Pork Shoulder with
White Beans and Chard (page 209)

I love crunchy fruit in salads, which is why I suggest you seek out slightly underripe Fuyu persimmons here. If you can't find them, feel free to substitute Asian pears or more regular apples (a mix of all three would not be bad, either). You want the fruit to be fairly acidic and salty; the honey is there to compensate for any lack of naturally occurring sweetness, so adjust with more as needed.

Fresh horseradish is one of my favorite niche ingredients that I don't love to call for because I know it can be challenging to find, but I have noticed it increasingly pop up at grocery stores, so I'm just going to live my truth and call for it. If you can't find it, prepared horseradish will do the trick—just expect a tangier salad (not the worst thing).

1 Arrange the apples and persimmons on a large serving plate. Drizzle with the vinegar and honey (if using prepared horseradish, mix with vinegar and honey first so that you can evenly distribute), and sprinkle with flaky salt and pepper. Give everything a subtle toss, being gentle to avoid breakage. Season with more salt, pepper, honey, and vinegar as needed.

2 Using a peeler, shave a bit of horseradish onto the fruit, followed by a crumbling of the cheese. Drizzle all over with olive oil before serving.

Crushed Peas with Burrata and Black Olives

serves 4 to 6

¼ cup oil-cured black olives or
  Castelvetrano olives, pitted
⅓ cup olive oil
2 cups fresh (or frozen, thawed!)
  English peas
2 tablespoons freshly grated
  lemon zest
Kosher salt and freshly ground
  black pepper
3 cups spicy greens, such as
  mustard greens or arugula
1 cup fresh mint leaves, torn
2 tablespoons finely chopped
  fresh chives
½ cup fresh parsley, tender leaves
  and stems
2 tablespoons fresh lemon juice,
  plus more to taste
2 balls burrata cheese, drained
  (you can also use mozzarella; just
  expect a different visual)

EAT WITH
Melon with Crispy Ham and Ricotta
Salata (page 114)
+
Sungold Pasta with Lemony Shellfish,
Garlic, and Pistachios (page 250)

I'm sure you've already figured this out, but I'll say it anyway. This "salad" is just an excuse to eat an extraordinary amount of cheese. It's also a way to eat an extraordinary amount of peas, which I love. For what it's worth, I am not the kind of person who insists on shelling in-season, farmers' market peas (I think frozen peas are pretty damn good and can absolutely be used here), but if you happen upon them, there is no dish more worthy of the glory of fresh peas than this one.

1 Combine the olives and olive oil in a small bowl; set aside.

2 Place half of the peas in a medium bowl. Using your hands (or, if you're more refined and/or own one, a potato masher), crush the peas. You're looking for crushed, not a puree, so don't bother using a food processor. Add the remaining peas and lemon zest, and season with salt and pepper.

3 Toss the greens, mint, chives, parsley, and lemon juice together in another medium bowl, and season with salt and pepper and a bit more lemon juice if you like.

4 Tear the burrata into pieces and arrange on a large serving platter or in a shallow bowl (you can also cut the burrata, but tearing it is much easier). Scatter the crushed peas on and around the burrata and top with the olive mixture, followed by the spicy greens and herbs.

DO AHEAD Peas can be seasoned a day ahead, covered tightly, and stored in the refrigerator.

Smashed Cucumbers with Sizzled Turmeric and Garlic

serves 4 to 6

½ cup grapeseed oil

6 garlic cloves, coarsely chopped

1-inch knob fresh turmeric, coarsely
  chopped, or ½ teaspoon ground
  turmeric

1 teaspoon flaky sea salt, plus more
  for seasoning

6 Persian cucumbers, or 2 hothouse
  cucumbers, cut into 1-inch chunks

2 scallions or 1 spring onion, green
  and white parts, thinly sliced

3 tablespoons distilled white vinegar,
  white wine vinegar, or rice wine
  vinegar, plus more to taste

Freshly ground black pepper

½ cup fresh mixed herbs,
  such as dill and mint, tender
  leaves and stems

EAT WITH
Buttered Turmeric Rice with Crushed
Almonds and Herbs (page 173)
+
Soy-Braised Brisket with Caramelized
Honey and Garlic (page 226)

Smashing cucumbers is not just a fun thing to do and say, but it also serves a purpose. Since they are mostly water, it's best to salt and then smash them, which releases some of the water and concentrates those cucumber flavors. What you're left with is a crunchy, craggily, geode-esque vegetable, ready to be graced by an assertively delicious dressing.

Here, that dressing starts with a toasted garlic oil laced with turmeric, not just for color (although, would you *look* at that color??) but for its vaguely ginger-y, deeply earthy flavor, which loves a cucumber.

It's hard to say how this salad-y number is best served—because the answer is "with everything and all the time."

1 Heat the oil in a medium pot over medium heat. Add the garlic and cook, swirling the pot occasionally, until the garlic is sizzling loudly and looks (and smells) delightfully toasted, 2 to 3 minutes. Add the turmeric and flaky salt and swirl the pot. Remove from the heat; set aside.

2 Place the cucumbers in a large resealable plastic bag and season with salt. Using a heavy skillet, rolling pin, or anything heavy, smash the cucumbers until they split and explode a bit. Let them sit few minutes to release some of that water.

3 Drain the cucumbers, discarding any liquid. Combine the cucumbers, scallions, and vinegar in a large serving bowl. Season with salt, pepper, and more vinegar. Drizzle with the toasted garlic oil, letting it run into the tiny scraggly bits. Scatter with the herbs before serving.

DO AHEAD Cucumbers can be smashed a few hours ahead, draining and seasoning before serving. Crunchy garlic and turmeric oil can be made 2 days ahead, covered, and refrigerated; bring to room temperature before using.

Summer Squash with Basil, Parmesan, and Toasted Buckwheat

serves 4 to 6

2 tablespoons buckwheat kernels (also unfortunately known as buckwheat groats) or pumpkin seeds

2 medium summer squash (about 1¼ pounds), very thinly sliced

3 tablespoons fresh lemon juice

1 teaspoon fish sauce

Kosher salt and freshly ground black pepper

1 good hunk of parmesan cheese, for grating

Olive oil, for drizzling

¼ cup finely chopped fresh chives

¼ cup fresh basil leaves, torn

¼ cup fresh parsley, tender leaves and stems

EAT WITH
Roasted Radishes with Green Goddess Butter (page 124)
+
Grilled Trout with Green Goddess Butter (page 244)

Summer squash is, admittedly, pretty boring. It doesn't taste like a whole lot and is made mostly of water. So what's it doing here? I would not steer you wrong—hear me out. It's so wildly abundant in the summer that I feel guilty not cooking with it (don't you?), so I'm always trying new ways to attempt to love this vegetable. Turns out, if you dress it with enough fresh lemon juice and salty fish sauce, and blanket it with Parmesan cheese, oniony chives, and very crunchy things like buckwheat, it's better than tolerable—it's amazing.

1 Toast the buckwheat in a small skillet over medium heat, tossing frequently until golden brown and starting to smell like popcorn, 2 to 3 minutes. Remove from the heat and set aside.

2 Toss the squash with the lemon juice and fish sauce in a large bowl, and season with salt and pepper. Scatter the squash on a large serving platter or in a shallow bowl. Grate the parmesan over, drizzle with olive oil, and top with the buckwheat, chives, basil, and parsley.

DO AHEAD I would not do anything ahead of time here, other than toast the buckwheat or pumpkin seeds. This salad is best dressed when you're ready to serve and eat it. (After it's dressed it begins to lose texture and flavor, so it's kind of a dress-and-eat situation.)

Tomatoes Dressed in Toasted Fennel and Anchovy

serves 4 to 8

½ cup olive oil

2 tablespoons fennel seeds, crushed

2 teaspoons Aleppo-style pepper, or 1 teaspoon crushed red pepper flakes

8 anchovy fillets, plus more if you like

2–3 pounds small-ish very ripe tomatoes, quartered or sliced

2 tablespoons red wine vinegar or white wine vinegar

Flaky sea salt

Coarsely ground black pepper

EAT WITH
Celery and Fennel with Walnuts and Blue Cheese (page 95)
+
Swordfish with Crushed Olives and Oregano (page 243)

Ever eat something so good it makes you cry? This happens to me, mostly when I'm in an exotic locale eating something exquisite—like Portugal (grilled head-on prawns tossed with garlic and olive oil) or Rome (*cacio e pepe*, obviously)—but it rarely happens with food I make because I'm too close to it. Though, the first time I made these tomatoes, cooking with friends in some fantasy upstate house (that definitely did not belong to any of us), there were tears (of joy!).

You're probably thinking that you need perfect tomatoes to make this dish, but the beauty is that you don't (any East Coaster will tell you that the good tomatoes don't even show up until late August). The insanely flavorful oil used to dress them, spicy from pepper flakes, crunchy with toasted fennel seed, and salty with bits of anchovy, will transform any tomato. It's also good on most vegetables—raw summer squash, cucumbers, radish or fennel, roasted eggplant, sautéed greens or broccoli . . . I could go on. Okay, I will. Its also good tossed with pasta, to dip bread in, spooned over creamy goat cheese or feta, or . . . you get the idea.

1 Heat the olive oil in a small pot over medium heat. Add the fennel seeds, Aleppo-style pepper, and anchovies, swirling and toasting until the spices are fragrant and the anchovies are melted, 2 to 4 minutes. Remove from the heat and set aside.

2 Scatter the tomatoes on a large serving platter or in a shallow bowl. Drizzle with the vinegar and, if you want, scatter with more anchovies (or just serve alongside in their little tin for snacking on). Spoon the toasted fennel–anchovy mixture over and top with flaky salt and a few grinds of black pepper.

DO AHEAD The toasted fennel–anchovy oil can be made up to 2 weeks ahead, tightly covered, and stored in the refrigerator. The tomatoes can be sliced 1 hour ahead, if you must, but are really best if sliced, dressed, and served immediately.

Charred Corn and Scallions with Tomatillo

serves 4 to 6

1 bunch scallions or spring onions

6 ears fresh corn, shucked

2 tablespoons canola or
   grapeseed oil

Kosher salt and freshly ground black
   pepper

2 tablespoons fresh lime juice

4 tomatillos, husked and rinsed,
   thinly sliced

1 cup fresh cilantro, tender leaves
   and stems, coarsely chopped,
   plus more for garnish

1–2 avocados, depending on how
   much you like avocado, sliced or
   coarsely chopped (optional)

Olive oil, for drizzling

NOTE *I mention avocados
to give you permission to use
them, because I know you
probably want to. Logically,
I know they would be great,
but avocados make me feel
nothing, so I leave them
"optional."*

EAT WITH
Other grilled dishes, such as Grilled
Shrimp with Crushed Fresh Tomatoes
and Lots of Lime (page 232)
+
Citrus Chicken Rested in Herbs
(page 214)

This salad is the best thing about a corn salsa without (a) calling it a corn salsa; and (b) using tomatoes, which I find too wet and too soft for this kind of thing. The tomatillos, by comparison, are firm, super tart, and have just the right amount of juiciness—enough to act as a sort of dressing for the charred corn without making everything soggy (the worst!). I think corn is the best version of itself when grilled (the sugars in the corn caramelize just like sugar in a pan does), but blasting it in a very hot oven is a great alternative. (For a photo of the finished dish, see page 230.)

1 Heat a grill to high heat (or preheat the oven to 500°F).

2 Finely chop 2 scallions, green and white parts; set aside. Place the corn and whole scallions on a large rimmed baking sheet; drizzle with the oil and season with salt and pepper.

3 Grill the corn until deeply charred on all sides (the best way to do this is by letting the ears char without moving them, rotating only every few minutes or so), 8 to 10 minutes. Add the scallions and grill about a minute or two. (If using the oven, simply roast, turning occasionally, until the corn and scallions are golden brown and lightly charred, 15 to 20 minutes. The corn will never char as if it had been grilled, but this is okay; get as much color as possible.) Let corn cool slightly.

4 Using a sharp knife, remove the kernels from the corn and place in a large bowl along with the lime juice, tomatillos, and cilantro. Coarsely chop the charred scallions and add to the corn along with the remaining raw chopped scallions. Toss to coat and season with salt and pepper.

5 Transfer to a large bowl or serving platter, top with more cilantro and avocado, if desired, and drizzle with olive oil.

DO AHEAD Corn salad can be made a day ahead, stored in a container, and refrigerated.

Melon with Crispy Ham and Ricotta Salata

serves 4 to 8

4 ounces thinly sliced prosciutto, speck, or coppa ham

1 cantaloupe or other melon, cut into thin wedges, peel removed if you like

1 lemon, cut in half crosswise

Flaky sea salt

2 ounces ricotta salata or firm mild feta, very thinly sliced

Olive oil, for drizzling

Freshly ground black pepper

NOTE *If you're making this as a snack, serve it with dips as part of a "not-crudité" platter (page 54), or alongside other crispy, crunchy, salty things like the breadsticks on page 66 or giant crunchy corn on page 74.*

If you're thinking *Is this just ham and melon together?*, well, the answer is, yes, there is ham and there is melon, but the ham is crispy and the melon is tangy, so let's just say that this is a whole different ball game from prosciutto-wrapped melon. Oh, there is also cheese, making it a real one-stop-shopping kind of scene. More salad than snack, but truthfully, it can be eaten as either a predinner snack or a dinner salad. The only thing that would change is your plating: for a snack, the ingredients can be cut a bit larger and casually draped over one another; for a salad, they should be a touch more bite-sized and casually tossed together.

There are only two rules for this dish: (1) Your melon, as when eating any melon, should be as ripe and delicious as possible; I'm talking juices running down your forearm ripe. (2) Make sure to assemble the salad just before serving, so that the ham stays crispy as intended.

1 Preheat the oven to 425°F. Line a rimmed baking sheet with parchment paper. Lay the prosciutto in a thin, even layer (without overlapping or touching) and bake until crispy and crunchy (it may wrinkle and crinkle a bit, that's okay), 8 to 12 minutes. Remove from the heat and set aside.

2 Arrange the melon wedges on a large platter and squeeze lemon juice all over. Sprinkle with the salt.

3 On a serving plate, scatter the ricotta salata and ham bits around. Drizzle with olive oil and give it a good few grinds of fresh pepper before serving.

DO AHEAD Ham can be crisped 2 days ahead. Store covered at room temperature.

sides

"Side dish" is a very misleading term.

It implies something that exists only to serve as an accompaniment to something else. No disrespect to a great chicken or an expensive steak, but it's no secret that sides are often the most delicious thing on the table. In fact, I make a meal of "just sides" all the time and don't see anything wrong with your doing that, either. Side dishes deserve our unrestrained love and utmost respect! Thank you for coming to my TED Talk.

Anyway, if salads bring their bright, clean, tangy texture, sides provide a hearty, starchy, warm, comforting moment. They can be anchored by vegetables prepared literally every way (Steamed! Grilled! Roasted! Sautéed!), served spicy or saucy or both. Sides can be a pot of well-cooked grains tossed with caramelized fennel (page 164) or a few cans of rinsed legumes crisped up in olive oil with feta and oregano (page 168). A creamy cauliflower gratin (page 151) is a side and so is a platter of halved long-roasted eggplant with crunchy, garlicky bread crumbs (page 158). If there was a time for butter, extra carbs, and lots of cheese, sides are it (but don't forget to finish with lemon and plenty of fresh herbs to stay on brand here, okay?).

Mustardy Green Beans with Anchovyed Walnuts

serves 4 to 6

1 cup raw walnuts, coarsely chopped

½ cup plus 2 tablespoons olive oil, divided, plus more for drizzling

4 anchovy fillets

1 garlic clove, finely grated

1½ pounds fresh green beans, trimmed

1 lemon, thinly sliced, seeds removed

Kosher salt and freshly ground black pepper

2 tablespoons whole-grain mustard

1 tablespoon distilled white vinegar or white wine vinegar

¼ cup fresh dill, finely chopped

I'm rarely ambivalent about anything, but right now I'll level with you. When it comes to this particular recipe, it doesn't really matter how you cook the green beans. The key is to have just-cooked green beans, lightly dressed and topped in a tangy, mustardy dressing, with toasted, garlicky, anchovyed walnuts. The most interesting way to cook the beans in my opinion is grilling, because you can do it hot and fast so they get nicely charred without overcooking, but unless you have fat green beans or a grill with small grates, it can be heartbreaking (and annoying) to watch them slip through and fall into the coals. That said, roasting is great, especially when cooking for a crowd because you can roast a lot at a time in only a few minutes (just make sure not to crowd the baking sheet). That also said, I mean, if you want to just sauté them, you can do that, too! It's honestly a real "choose your own green bean adventure."

1 Preheat the oven to 450°F (or heat a grill to medium-high).

2 Heat the walnuts and ¼ cup oil in a medium pot over medium heat. Cook, swirling occasionally, until the walnuts are toasted, 2 to 3 minutes. Remove from the heat and add the anchovies and garlic, swirling to dissolve the anchovies; set aside.

3 Place the green beans and lemon on a rimmed baking sheet and drizzle with enough olive oil to lightly coat and season with salt and pepper. Roast (or grill), tossing green beans and lemon once or twice, until they've started to char and brown in spots, 12 to 15 minutes (closer to 8 to 10 if grilling).

4 Combine the mustard, vinegar, and the remaining ¼ cup olive oil in a large bowl and season with salt and pepper. Add the green beans and toss to coat. Transfer to a serving platter and top with the reserved walnuts and the dill.

DO AHEAD Green beans can be cooked and dressed a few hours ahead, stored loosely covered at room temperature (this is an excellent room-temperature dish).

Grilled Carrots with Limey Hot Sauce and Cotija

serves 4 to 6

1½ pounds small to medium carrots, scrubbed and halved lengthwise

3 tablespoons olive oil, plus more for drizzling

Kosher salt and freshly ground black pepper

¼ cup fresh lime juice

½ jalapeño, seeds removed if you want less heat, finely chopped

1 small garlic clove, finely grated

2 teaspoons honey

1 cup fresh cilantro, tender leaves and stems

1–2 ounces cotija or crumbled queso fresco, mild feta, or ricotta salata

NOTE *These carrots are almost better at room temperature (or even cold) so if you're grilling something else (like the chicken on page 214), throw these on first and let them hang out while you do everything else.*

Grilled corn is good, yes, but have you ever had a grilled carrot? Super high in sugar content, the carrot caramelizes and chars like no other and cooks in a fraction of the time corn does (because, you know, smaller circumference and all). Of course, you don't *have* to grill these carrots, but grilled carrots are good as hell, and if you have the opportunity to do so, grill 'em. (Don't worry, they are just as delicious roasted in a hot oven.)

No matter how you get there, the moral of the story is you're charring and crisping carrots, dousing them in a slightly sweet, very limey, kinda spicy sauce and then sprinkling them with cheese, making yourself and anyone you feed them to extremely happy.

1. Heat a grill to medium-high (or heat the oven to 450°F).

2 Toss the carrots on a rimmed baking sheet with the olive oil and season with salt and pepper. Grill (or roast), turning occasionally, until the carrots are deeply browned and caramelized on all sides, 8 to 10 minutes (15 to 20 minutes in the oven). Remove from the grill and let cool slightly.

3 Meanwhile, combine the lime juice, jalapeño, garlic, and honey in a small bowl; season with salt and pepper.

4 Place the carrots on a large serving platter or plate and drizzle with a bit of olive oil. Spoon the limey hot sauce over and scatter with the cilantro and cotija, serving any remaining hot sauce alongside for serving, dipping, etc.

DO AHEAD Carrots can be cooked up to 2 days ahead (they are excellent cold), covered tightly, and refrigerated.

Roasted Radishes with Green Goddess Butter

serves 4 to 6

FOR THE GREEN GODDESS BUTTER

½ cup (1 stick) unsalted butter, room temperature

½ cup fresh parsley, tender leaves and stems, very finely chopped

¼ cup fresh tarragon leaves, very finely chopped

¼ cup very finely chopped fresh chives

4 anchovy fillets, very finely chopped

1 garlic clove, finely grated

2 tablespoons white wine vinegar

Kosher salt and freshly ground black pepper

FOR THE VEGETABLES

2 bunches radishes or baby turnips with tops on, scrubbed well and halved lengthwise

3 tablespoons olive oil

1 lemon, halved

Flaky sea salt

Freshly ground black pepper

If you thought I was going to write a book and not include yet another variation on the world's two most perfect ingredients together (radishes and butter), then you were mistaken. These radishes are roasted hot and fast, with their tops on, so you get a nice, golden brown and tender radish (which tastes like a turnip, if you ask me), and crispy, crunchy tops (which taste like kale chips, if you also ask me). When they come out of the oven, they get laid on a bed of herby, garlicky, anchovy-rich butter, which will slightly melt under the residual heat of the vegetables but generally stays creamy, ideal for dipping, swooping, and scooping.

If you have extra Green Goddess Butter (and you will), serve it over seared steak, swordfish (page 243), whole fish (page 244), chicken, or on toast, melted into pasta, on a spoon directly into your mouth, and so on. It's so versatile and delicious, you'll want to put it on everything.

1 Make the Green Goddess Butter. Combine the butter, parsley, tarragon, chives, anchovies, garlic, and vinegar in a medium bowl. Smash with a fork until well blended (alternatively, place all ingredients in a food processor and blend until well combined). Season with salt and pepper.

2 Preheat the oven to 425°F.

3 Prepare the vegetables. Toss the radishes and olive oil together on a rimmed baking sheet, making sure to get olive oil on the leaves as well. Roast until the radishes are tender and the tops are browned and crispy, 12 to 15 minutes.

4 Spread the Green Goddess Butter on a serving plate or in a shallow bowl. Top with the radishes and squeeze lemon juice over everything. Sprinkle with flaky salt and pepper and serve.

DO AHEAD Green Goddess Butter can be made up to 2 weeks ahead, covered tightly, and refrigerated. Bring the butter to room temperature before serving.

Wine-Roasted Artichokes

serves 4 to 6

2–3 large artichokes (1½–2 pounds
    total)
1 cup white wine
1 cup water
¼ cup olive oil
4 tablespoons (½ stick) unsalted
    butter, cut into ½-inch pieces
4 garlic cloves, smashed
Pinch of crushed red pepper flakes
    (optional)
Kosher salt and freshly ground black
    pepper
Lemony Aioli (page 37), optional

EAT WITH
Escarole with Mustard and Spicy
Guanciale Bread Crumbs (page 82)
+
Halibut with Asparagus and Brown-
Buttered Peas (page 237)

This recipe involves a bit of good news and a bit of bad news. Which do you want first? I'll go ahead with the good news: Once these artichokes are cooked in their oily, white wine bath, you can eat them without teaching anyone how to navigate the thorny beast or deal with the feathery choke. The bad news: You have to clean them while they are raw, which, depending on how much you've had to drink, could be at worst dangerous and at best pretty annoying. So why am I telling you to do it that way? Because it's worth it. Hey—at least I'm not asking you to deep-fry anything.

The two-step cooking process achieves two things. First, you steam the artichokes covered in foil until tender, making each leaf down to the heart soft and edible (do not skip this part, or the leaves will not be soft enough to eat). Second, you uncover the artichokes to evaporate the excess liquid, and caramelize the bottom, and you get the outer leaves all crispy, which are so good for nibbling on (do not skip this part, or the whole thing will not be as delicious).

Seasoned with acidic white wine from the inside out, these artichokes need nothing more than the garlicky oil they've sizzled in for dipping, but I am a "more is more" person when it comes to artichokes and would welcome a lemony aioli or creamy labne, as well.

1 Preheat the oven to 425°F.

2 Trim the very ends of the artichoke stem, but leave most of it (it's an extension of the heart and will taste just as good). Using a serrated knife, slice the first 1½ inches off the top, exposing the yellow-y purple rose-like interior. Using your hands, peel away the first two to three layers of those tough, dark green outer leaves, leaving the most tender, paler green ones behind. Using kitchen scissors, trim any lingering thorns on the leaves.

3 Cut the artichokes in half lengthwise. Using a spoon, dig out the fuzzy choke of each half, making sure to scrape clean any lingering bits. Place the artichokes, cut side down, in a large baking dish (size will depend on whether you're doing 2 or 3, but a 9 by 13-inch pan should do the trick either way). Don't worry about storing them in acidulated water to prevent browning—they are going to brown regardless once you roast them, so who cares? I never really understood this.

4 Pour the wine, water, and olive oil over the artichokes. Add the butter, garlic, and crushed red pepper flakes, if using; season everything with salt and pepper. (Remember you're seasoning the artichokes and the cooking liquid, so be generous.) Cover tightly with foil and roast until the artichokes are totally tender, 45 to 55 minutes.

5 Remove the foil and continue to roast until the liquid is mostly evaporated (the olive oil will linger behind), the tops of the artichokes are nicely browned, and the garlic begins to sizzle and brown in the olive oil (the cut sides of the artichokes will also be sizzling and browning), another 15 to 20 minutes.

6 Transfer the antichokes to a large serving platter or bowl. Scrape any of the garlicky oil at the bottom of the baking dish into a small bowl for serving alongside the aioli, if you like.

DO AHEAD Artichokes can be roasted a few hours ahead, kept loosely covered at room temperature. There is no need to reheat before serving, but you can definitely pop them into a hot oven for a bit to warm them through, if you like.

Harissa-Braised Green Beans with Herbs

serves 6

2 tablespoons olive oil, plus more
 as needed
2 tablespoons harissa paste
4 garlic cloves, smashed
1 large ripe tomato, quartered
Kosher salt and freshly ground black
 pepper
¼ cup dry white wine
1½ pounds fresh romano, wax, or
 green beans, stems trimmed
1 cup mixed tender fresh herbs,
 such as parsley, cilantro, dill,
 and/or mint
½ cup finely chopped fresh chives
2 tablespoons finely grated
 lemon zest

EAT WITH
Summer Squash with Basil, Parmesan,
and Toasted Buckwheat (page 108)
+
Grilled Lamb Shoulder over Fresh
Garlicky Tomatoes (page 206)

I have a few unwavering preferences including, but not limited to: I will never be a morning person, I will never use a top sheet, and I prefer my vegetables crispy. The last one means I'm almost always roasting my vegetables hot and fast, or grilling them even hotter and faster.

But once in a while a person, dish, or moment changes my mind (although I will *never* use a top sheet!). Recently, my friend Amiel told me how he loves to "cook the shit out of" his vegetables, long and slow, beating every ounce of texture out of them until they're lifeless and soft and flavorless, probably. *I mean, sure, dude! Sounds not good!* I thought. But then he stewed a pot of them (for one million years), until they were fall-apart tender and, yes, intensely flavorful. Because I can admit when I'm wrong I'll tell you (and him): a stewed green bean can be just as good as a crisp, barely cooked one.

That said, I still prefer a bit of "al dente" texture, so my version of "braised long and slow" is only about 30 minutes. This way, they maintain their lovely green color and touch of snap but still qualify as tender.

1 Heat the olive oil in a medium pot over medium heat. Add the harissa and garlic, and cook, stirring occasionally, until the harissa has started to caramelize, 2 to 3 minutes. Add the tomato and season with salt and pepper. Cook until the tomato begins to break down into a pulpy mash, 3 to 4 minutes. Add the wine and cook until reduced by about half, 2-ish minutes.

2 Add the beans and stir to coat in the spicy tomato-y business. Season with salt and pepper, reduce the heat to medium-low, and place the lid on top. Let them do their thing in there for 15 to 20 minutes before stirring. Continue cooking until the beans are starting to turn a more olive, army green color and are delightfully softened but not yet mushy, 10 to 15 minutes more. Top with the herbs and lemon zest before serving.

DO AHEAD Green beans can be made 2 days ahead, kept tightly covered and refrigerated; gently rewarm before serving.

Sticky Roasted Carrots with Citrus and Tahini

serves 4 to 6

1 small or ½ medium red onion, peeled and cut into ½-inch wedges

2 tablespoons fresh lemon or lime juice, plus more for seasoning

Kosher salt and freshly ground black pepper

2 bunches small carrots (about 1 pound), tops removed, scrubbed, quartered lengthwise

1 small, unpeeled blood orange, tangerine, or lemon, thinly sliced, seeds removed

4 chiles de arbol, lightly crushed, or ½ teaspoon crushed red pepper flakes

2 tablespoons pure maple syrup or honey

¼ cup olive oil, plus more for drizzling

¼ cup tahini

3 tablespoons water

EAT WITH
Lemony Watercress with Raw and Toasted Fennel (page 87)
+
Spiced and Braised Short Ribs with Creamy Potatoes (page 224)

Roasted carrots are sweet enough that they don't really need much help in that department, but I still like adding maple syrup or honey when roasting because I love how they get all shiny and sticky. The perfect thing to do here is to channel the powers of an excellent PB&J and smear a bit of seasoned nutty tahini sauce (the peanut butter, naturally) on the bottom of the plate, then eat those sticky carrots with some jammy, roasted citrus slices (the jelly, of course). To keep things decidedly savory, the carrots are also roasted with red onion that's taken a bath in lemon juice, because the only thing better than a roasted onion is a roasted pickled onion.

1 Preheat the oven to 425°F.

2 Toss the onion and lemon juice together in a small bowl. Season with salt and pepper and let sit 8 to 10 minutes to lightly pickle.

3 Drain the onion, discarding the liquid. On a rimmed baking sheet, toss the onion with the carrots, orange, chiles, maple syrup, and olive oil.

4 Roast, tossing occasionally until the carrots and citrus slices are totally tender and caramelized at the ends, 25 to 30 minutes.

5 Meanwhile, combine the tahini and water in a small bowl; season with salt and pepper.

6 Spoon some of the tahini sauce on the bottom of a large serving platter or plate and top with the carrots, onion, and citrus. Serve extra tahini sauce alongside.

DO AHEAD Carrots and citrus can be roasted a few hours ahead, kept loosely wrapped until ready to serve (no need to reheat). Tahini sauce can be made 1 week ahead, kept in a sealed container and refrigerated.

Crushed Baby Potatoes with Scallion, Celery, and Lots of Dill

serves 4 to 6

1½ pounds small, waxy potatoes, such as golden creamers or fingerlings (preferably the size of a golf ball, no larger than a tangerine)

Kosher salt

⅓ cup olive oil

¼ cup finely chopped fresh dill, plus more for garnish

1 tablespoon finely grated lemon zest

2 tablespoons fresh lemon juice, plus more as needed

4 scallions, white and green parts, thinly sliced

Coarsely ground black pepper

4 celery stalks, thinly sliced on the bias

1 cup celery leaves or tender leaves and stems of fresh parsley

1 tin of sardines, anchovy fillets, or other fish of your dreams, torn or cut into bite-sized pieces (optional, but come on)

I love to keep boiled potatoes around for out-of-hand snacking, to place on my platter of "thoughtfully arranged vegetables" (page 54), and as a quick addition to things like a skillet full of chicken fat. But aside from the crispy kind, there is no better application for smashed boiled potatoes than a potato-y salad. No, not potato salad, a potato-y salad. (Calling this a "potato-y salad" allows me the freedom to express myself without judgment since defining potato salad really gets people riled up—Mayonnaise? *No mayonnaise!* Celery? *Always!*).

Here, the potatoes are crushed so the chunkiness (for texture) can coexist with the more broken-up pieces (for creaminess) while those exposed craggy edges absorb that lemony, scalliony, salty dressing. The tinned fish are optional, but they are truly good in this application—little pieces of fatty, salty fish to be snacked on between bites of dilly, tangy potatoes and crunchy celery.

1 Boil the potatoes in salted water until they're completely tender, 10 to 15 minutes depending on the size of the potato. Drain and let sit until they're cool enough to lightly crush with the palms of your hands.

2 Meanwhile, combine the olive oil, dill, lemon zest, lemon juice, and half the scallions in a small bowl; season with salt and pepper and more lemon juice.

3 Add the crushed potatoes and celery and toss to coat; season with salt and pepper.

4 Transfer the potatoes, celery, and any dressing to a large serving platter. Top with the celery leaves, remaining scallions, more dill, and more pepper. Serve with sardines or anchovies alongside or scattered over.

DO AHEAD Potatoes can be boiled up to 1 week ahead, covered, and refrigerated. Potato salad can be made up to 2 days ahead, covered, and refrigerated.

Smashed Sweet Potatoes
with Maple and Sour Cream

serves 4 to 6

1½ pounds small sweet potatoes
 (about 4–6)
1 cup sour cream
2 tablespoons fresh lime or lemon
 juice
Kosher salt and freshly ground black
 pepper
2 tablespoons olive oil
6 tablespoons (¾ stick) unsalted
 butter
⅓ cup pure maple syrup
¼ cup toasted buckwheat groats
 (kasha)
2 tablespoons fresh thyme leaves
Flaky sea salt

EAT WITH
Little Gems with Garlicky Lemon and
Pistachio (page 88)
+
One-Pot Chicken with Dates and
Caramelized Lemon (page 194)

Following in the great tradition of crispy smashed potatoes, these potatoes are also twice cooked, but with different results (because a sweet potato, after all, is not a regular potato). Less crispy than its starchy friend, this is more about the creamy interior than the crispy exterior.

You can, of course, use larger sweet potatoes, but I will say that the final product will not be as adorable.

1 Preheat the oven to 400°F.

2 Using a fork, prick the sweet potatoes all over so that they don't explode in the oven (which might happen!). Place directly on the wire rack and bake until totally tender, 50 to 60 minutes. Remove from the oven to cool.

3 Meanwhile, combine the sour cream and lime juice and season with salt and pepper. It should be fairly tart and salty. Smear on the bottom of a serving platter.

4 Once the potatoes are cool enough to handle, use the palm of your hand to crush them slightly.

5 Heat the olive oil and butter in a large skillet over medium heat. Working in batches, add the potatoes, pressing lightly to make contact with the skillet. Season with salt and pepper and cook until lightly crisped and browned on one side, 3 to 4 minutes. Flip and continue to cook until browned and crisped on the other side. Transfer potatoes to the serving platter and repeat with any stragglers.

6 Without wiping out the skillet, add the maple syrup and cook until it's thickened and starting to caramelize, about 2 minutes. Pour all over the sweet potatoes. Top with the buckwheat, thyme, and lots of flaky salt.

DO AHEAD Sweet potatoes can be baked up to 5 days ahead, covered, and refrigerated.

steamed broccoli: a love letter

Steamed broccoli is awesome. Not since "I love boiled potatoes" have I written something so boring, but there you have it. Now, let me take up an entire page telling you why.

Finding a vegetable that is as good blanched or steamed as it is roasted or grilled is a true miracle and something that should be celebrated. Broccoli and all its affiliates—broccoli rabe, baby broccoli, broccolini—manage to shine in nearly all applications, but I can say with total honesty that on many occasions, especially when it relates to a table full of food, I prefer it blanched or steamed—even more so when it gets assaulted with an insane amount of fresh lemon juice, drizzled with a good amount of olive oil, and sprinkled with crunchy, flaky sea salt.

It doesn't need much more than that. In fact, resist the urge to sprinkle with cheese or drag through a pool of sour cream. Both of those would be very good, obviously, but the beauty here is in picking up an assertively lemoned neon-green stalk and popping it all into your mouth in between bites of cheesy pasta or brothy, braised meat. It's the palate cleanser (made of broccoli) you never knew you needed, until now.

TO MAKE

Vis-á-vis blanching or steaming, which route I'll take largely depends on what else I'm doing. For example, if I'm making pasta that night, I'll blanch the broccoli in the pasta water before I add my pasta (sure, the water turns a little green, but my pasta doesn't seem to care—just make sure the water is plenty salted!). If I'm braising something in the oven, while I wait, I'll set up a little steam situation on top of the stove. Both are great.

To blanch, cook 1 to 1½ pounds (for 4 to 6 people) in a pot of salted boiling water until bright green and just tender (30 seconds or so for broccoli rabe, which is also great here, 60 seconds or so for baby broccoli, closer to 90 seconds for spears cut from a head of broccoli).

To steam, fill a large, wide pot with about 1½ inches water. Place a steamer basket in the pot, add the broccoli or broccoli rabe, and season with salt. Steam until bright green and just tender (60 seconds or so for broccoli rabe, 2 minutes or so for baby broccoli, closer to 4 minutes for spears cut from a head of broccoli).

From there, the key to making this truly excellent is make sure you really douse the broccoli in lemon once it's cooked. Do not hold back. It should be bracingly acidic, so much so that when you serve it to your friends, they might say, "Wow, that is SO lemony," and then find themselves unable to stop eating it. From there, sprinkle with flaky sea salt, a scattering of fresh herbs if you like, maybe a drizzle of olive oil, and a pinch of crushed red pepper flakes.

Spicy Caramelized Leeks with Fresh Lemon

serves 4 to 6

4 large leeks, dark green parts
    removed, halved lengthwise
⅓ cup olive oil
2 tablespoons harissa paste
Kosher salt and freshly ground black
    pepper
½ lemon, seeds removed, very finely
    chopped
Flaky sea salt

NOTE *Depending on where they are coming from, leeks can be dirty to quite dirty. Rinsing the halved leeks in a bowl of cold water is the best way to free them of dirt.*

I want to use this platform to issue a formal apology to leeks: Leeks, I've been ignoring you for years, almost always choosing literally any other allium over you. I'd like to think that those years of neglect were all in preparation for bringing us to this very moment, when you take center stage, shining in a dish that can only be described as "better than it ought to be," given the limited number of ingredients involved.

Here, leeks sizzle in a spicy olive oil mixture, the wild tendrilly ends crisping up like they've been deep fried, looking like an extremely festive and delicious party decoration; the pale green center becoming impossibly tender and creamy, finished with a bright raw lemon. If there was a dish to make you feel bad for ignoring leeks all this time, this is it. Don't worry—they forgive you!

1 Preheat the oven to 450°F.

2 Place the leeks cut side down and, without cutting through to the root, slice them lengthwise into ¼-inch strips. (You'll have a leek that looks like a streamer or palm fan). Place leeks in a 9 by 13-inch baking dish or on a rimmed baking sheet.

3 Whisk the olive oil and harissa together, then massage into the leeks, getting into all their layers. Season with salt and pepper and lay them straight-ish.

4 Roast, without disturbing too much so that they keep their long, wild shape, until they start to fry and sizzle and brown at the ends, 20 to 25 minutes.

5 Remove from the oven and transfer to a serving bowl or platter. Top with the lemon and flaky salt before serving.

DO AHEAD Leeks can be roasted several hours before serving, then kept loosely covered at room temperature. No need to reheat them before serving (they'll stay crispy and are good at room temperature), but you can if you like.

Just-Cooked Cabbage with Butter, Anchovy, and Lemon

serves 4 to 6

3 tablespoons olive oil, chicken fat, pork fat, or duck fat

1 large head of Savoy, cone, or white cabbage (do not use red or napa here), quartered lengthwise

Kosher salt and freshly ground black pepper

4–6 anchovy fillets

4 tablespoons (½ stick) unsalted butter

1 lemon, halved crosswise

Flaky sea salt

NOTE *Olive oil always works, but this is an excellent opportunity to use any leftover fat from something you may have just cooked in that same skillet (chicken thighs, pork chops, steak) to cook many vegetables, like fennel, mushrooms, garlic scapes, and radishes.*

This recipe almost didn't make it into the book, but after preparing it for a friend who is often my toughest critic, she demanded that it be included here, if only so she could cook it herself. Seared in a skillet until charred and tender, basted with butter and sizzled anchovies, and finished with a ridiculous amount of black pepper and fresh lemon, this cabbage is one of the most unsuspectingly delicious things in this book.

After eating an entire head of cabbage between the two of us, we both agreed that if more people had cabbage this good (and easy to make) cabbage would be a lot more popular. So here is this recipe, a last-minute gift from us to you, all in the name of spreading the cabbage gospel.

The key here is to stay true to the recipe name—which is to say, cook it just long enough so that it's *softened* but not *soft*. You'll know you've reached this point when the cabbage starts to kind of wilt onto itself but maintains its structure without totally collapsing into a pile of rags.

1 Heat your chosen fat in a large skillet, preferably cast-iron, over medium-high heat.

2 Season the cabbage with salt and pepper. Once the fat is super hot, add the cabbage, cut side down, and cook until it's well browned and caramelized, 4 to 6 minutes. Using tongs or a spatula, turn the cabbage and sear on the other cut side until it's just as browned and caramelized, 4 to 6 minutes. Transfer the cabbage to a large serving platter.

3 Add the anchovies and butter to the skillet, letting it foam up and get all browned while the anchovies melt into the fat, about 2 minutes.

4 Spoon the butter mixture over the cabbage and squeeze all over with both lemon halves. Sprinkle with flaky salt and pepper.

DO AHEAD This should be made right before you sit down to eat, which is to say, sorry, there are no do-aheads here!

my favorite bar is
a baked potato bar

Baked potatoes are underrated, and I want you to love them as much as I do. As with steamed artichokes, this is less of a recipe and more of a loud reminder that we should be making baked potatoes all the time, especially when having people over.

Now, I could see how if you've only known under-seasoned baked potatoes with soft skins and too few toppings, this idea might not excite you. However, I grew up eating the world's most perfect baked potatoes, made by my mom, who has an unrivaled preference for crispy things. Those potatoes were not microwaved (not because we were microwave averse but because it's impossible to get a crispy exterior on a potato by microwaving it), and definitely were not wrapped in foil (because how are they going to get crispy wrapped in foil?) but, rather, were rubbed in oil, seasoned with lots of salt, stabbed with a fork repeatedly and placed directly on the racks in a screaming-hot oven.

My mom and I waited at least an hour (even though it felt like five), and our patience was rewarded with a potato that was impossibly fluffy on the inside and shatteringly crispy on the outside. We'd crack them open, still steaming and too hot to eat, then smear them with large pats of butter, assault them with salt and freshly ground pepper, an absurd amount of chopped scallions, and, for my mom, sour cream (I didn't come to appreciate such an ingredient until later in life).

This "recipe" comes from her dad—my grandpa Bob—a true Renaissance man from Oklahoma, where he raised his own rabbits, grew his own tomatoes, baked his own bread, and, from what I hear, made the world's best baked potatoes. Now you get to, too.

Baked Potato Bar

serves 4 to 10

4–10 medium russet potatoes,
scrubbed well and patted dry
Canola oil
Kosher salt and freshly ground black
pepper

ACCEPTABLE TOPPINGS INCLUDE
BUT ARE NOT LIMITED TO
Sour cream, lots of it (sure, go
ahead and use Greek yogurt, but
don't blame me when you wish
you had used sour cream)
Chives and/or scallions, finely
chopped
Unsalted butter, preferably at room
temperature
Flaky sea salt and coarsely ground
black pepper
Trout or salmon roe (optional)
Finely chopped fresh dill and/or
parsley

NOTE *Don't cut the potatoes*
open until you're ready to eat
them or else the steam will
escape and they will lose heat
and the butter won't melt
when you put it on (a true
tragedy!).

While I frequently enjoy one for a solo dinner, baked potatoes are great when you're having people over. Not only are they about as crowd pleasing as it gets and require almost zero work on your part, but they are also the perfect opportunity to assemble a Really Cool Toppings Bar, a.k.a. the theme for my wedding, should I ever have one. Even though I find it hard to improve on the simple "lots of butter, salt, and too many scallions" combo, I do love to get dressed up for company and break out the picked herbs, sour cream, and fancy fish eggs. But don't let the presence of caviar intimidate you—the following are just suggestions, and do not have to be obeyed, by any means.

1 Preheat the oven to 500°F. This may seem excessive, but I assure you it is not.

2 Using a fork, poke the potatoes all around. This is kind of a violent act, I'll admit, but it's necessary so that the steam can escape the potato, allowing the inside to cook evenly and the skin to crisp. You could use a small knife, but I don't want anyone ending up in the hospital.

3 Drizzle a little oil onto each potato, or onto your hands, and just like you're oiling yourself up on some fantastic beach, rub the potatoes with a thin, even layer of oil. (My mom would do this with a paper towel; also an option.)

4 Season the potatoes on all sides with salt and pepper, and place directly onto the oven rack and bake until the potatoes are deeply crispy, dark, dark brown on the outside, and totally baked through, 60 to 70 minutes.

5 Carefully remove the potatoes and transfer to a large serving platter. Once ready to eat, slice them open lengthwise and fill to your heart's content with all the toppings in the land.

Roasted Squash with Yogurt and Spiced, Buttered Pistachios

serves 4 to 6

1 winter squash, such as Red Kuri, kabocha, or acorn, sliced into 1½-inch wedges (1½–2 pounds)

3 tablespoons olive oil

Kosher salt and freshly ground black pepper

6 tablespoons unsalted butter

¼ cup raw pistachios, finely chopped

½ teaspoon ground cumin

½ teaspoon ground turmeric

Pinch of ground cinnamon

Pinch of crushed red pepper flakes (optional)

Flaky sea salt

1 cup full-fat Greek yogurt

2 tablespoons fresh lemon juice

NOTE *Most winter squash works here, but my favorites are the larger, thick-skinned varieties such as Red Kuri, kabocha, and acorn, because you can eat the skin (and the seeds!). If using something like a butternut or honey nut, slice it into 1-inch-thick slices rather than wedges.*

For those on the East Coast, Winter Squash Season is a real "thing." At first, it's very exciting because it also means that it's Chunky Sweater Season and everyone is feeling extremely cozy, thrilled to be outside without sweating profusely. But soon you realize WSS lasts for approximately 84 years, and one month into it you might feel like dying if you have to eat one more roasted butternut.

The first time I made this it was peak WSS, and I still found myself shamelessly eating it with my hands, dragging each caramelized wedge through the lemony yogurt and buttery pistachios, swiping leftovers with my fingers, licking them clean like some sort of animal. Yes, it truly was that good.

1 Preheat the oven to 425°F.

2 Remove the seeds from the squash if you want (I leave them in, as I enjoy their crunchy texture as they roast, but whatever you like!) and toss the squash on a rimmed baking sheet with the olive oil. Season with salt and pepper, and roast until the squash is totally tender and golden brown with caramelized bits, 40 to 50 minutes.

3 Meanwhile, melt the butter in a small pot over medium heat. Cook, swirling occasionally, until the butter has browned and started to foam, 3 to 5 minutes. Remove from the heat and add the pistachios, cumin, turmeric, cinnamon, and red pepper flakes, if using. Season with flaky salt and set aside.

4 Combine the yogurt and lemon juice in a small bowl and season with salt. Spoon the yogurt sauce onto the bottom of a large serving platter or bowl. Arrange squash nestled into each other and spoon the buttered pistachios over everything. Top with flaky salt and a grind of black pepper or a pinch of red pepper flakes.

DO AHEAD Squash can be roasted several hours ahead of time, wrapped loosely, and stored at room temperature. It doesn't need to be reheated before serving, but you can if you like.

Hard-Roasted Spiced Cauliflower

serves 4 to 6

1 large head cauliflower, about
    2 pounds
4 garlic cloves, finely grated
1 teaspoon crushed red pepper
    flakes
1 teaspoon fennel seeds
½ teaspoon ground coriander
½ teaspoon ground turmeric
⅓ cup olive oil
Kosher salt and freshly ground black
    pepper
¼ cup finely chopped fresh chives,
    mint, parsley, or cilantro, tender
    leaves and stems (optional)
Crumbled feta, seasoned yogurt, or
    labne (optional)

NOTE *I find myself satisfied without the addition of crumbled feta or saucy yogurt here, but it's no secret that either would be super delicious served on top, underneath, or alongside.*

Something special happens to cauliflower when it's roasted for a very long time. It transforms from simply tender and soft to complexly crispy and toothsome, a word I really try to avoid using but sometimes can't. It's important to resist the urge to take out the cauliflower once it's just cooked through. You must push through, continuing to roast until the flavors have concentrated, the sugars have caramelized, the spices have toasted, and the bits have crisped.

The spices are light enough to vibe with nearly anything on your table, and this side dish can easily take the place of a grain or other starch. Not to complicate things, but you can even add a can of rinsed and drained chickpeas to the cauliflower before roasting. They'll cook and crisp along with the cauliflower, and then maybe you put a fried egg on top and serve with a crispy and crunchy salad, and then all of a sudden you have dinner.

1 Preheat the oven to 450°F.

2 Break the cauliflower into very small florets, about the size of a large bean. I just use my hands to do this, but you can use a knife.

3 Toss the cauliflower with the garlic, crushed red pepper flakes, fennel seeds, coriander, turmeric, and olive oil on a rimmed baking sheet and season with salt and lots and lots of pepper. Place in the oven and don't even think about touching it for at least 15 minutes. No, it won't burn! I promise.

4 After 15 minutes, toss the cauliflower occasionally to promote even browning, until each little friend is deeply browned and caramelized, another 15 to 20 minutes, with the smaller bits even darker and crispier (those are my favorite parts).

5 Transfer the cauliflower to a large platter and top with the herbs. Serve alongside feta, yogurt, or labne, if you just must.

DO AHEAD Cauliflower can be roasted a few hours ahead, covered loosely, and stored at room temperature.

Creamy Cauliflower and Onion Gratin

serves 6 to 10

1 cup heavy cream

4 tablespoons (½ stick) unsalted butter

2 garlic cloves, finely grated

Kosher salt and freshly ground black pepper

2½- to 3-pound cauliflower, leafy green parts removed

½ small sweet or yellow onion, very thinly sliced

6 ounces Gruyère or white cheddar cheese, grated (about 2½ cups)

Crushed red pepper flakes (optional)

2 cups fresh coarse bread crumbs (see page 14) or panko (optional)

3 tablespoons white sesame seeds

¼ cup olive oil (if using bread crumbs)

EAT WITH
Chicories with Preserved Lemon, Yogurt, and Mint (page 85)
+
Slow-Roasted Oregano Chicken with Buttered Tomatoes (page 189)

I am one of those people who'd never entertain the idea of replacing carbs with vegetables à la zoodles or cauliflower rice, but once this dish was born, I realized I was essentially using cauliflower as a replacement for pasta in this pasta-less version of what reminds me of macaroni and cheese. Believe me, I, too, was horrified, but it was so good that I did not and could not care.

This gratin is the easiest and most delicious way to make superlatively tender, creamy, cheesy cauliflower without any additional steps (no bechamel, roux, or other fancy sauce required). Bake the cauliflower, covered, in the cream, just to cook it through and get it tender, then uncover it so the cream can reduce, becoming thick and rich, and the cheese can get all browned and crispy.

It may seem like a crazy thing to do, but I left the bread crumbs optional for two reasons. One, because without them, it is a really great time for people who don't indulge in gluten to get on the gratin train (which is usually either bolstered with a roux made from flour, covered in nonnegotiable bread crumbs, or both); and two, I think this gratin is really, really good (and, superficially, more beautiful) without them. So good in fact, I couldn't choose between the two preparations, but would rather saddle you with this Sophie's Choice. Alternatively, make both versions and then decide for yourself.

1 Preheat the oven to 425°F.

2 Bring the cream, butter, and garlic to a simmer in a small pot over medium heat. Season with salt and pepper and remove from heat.

3 Slice the cauliflower into ½-inch-thick slabs (some of the bits will fall away and crumble into tiny florets; this is fine).

(recipe continues)

4 Place the smallest bits of cauliflower on the bottom of a 9-inch pie plate or cake pan (I like the roundness of the pie plates and cake pans, but a 2-quart baking dish of any shape will work). Scatter with some of the onion, followed by some of the cheese. Repeat with the remaining cauliflower, onion, and cheese until all of it is used, ending with the cheese.

5 Pour the cream mixture over (leave the garlic in or remove), followed by a good sprinkle of crushed red pepper flakes, if using.

6 Cover with aluminum foil and bake until the cauliflower is tender and cooked through, 20 to 25 minutes.

7 Remove the foil and continue to bake until the top is bubbly and golden and the cream is mostly reduced, another 15 to 20 minutes (it will look slightly runny and creamy in the oven but will set and thicken once you take it out of the oven and let it cool a few minutes).

8 If using the bread crumbs: Now is the time to put them to use. Combine the bread crumbs, sesame seeds, and olive oil in a medium bowl (alternatively, just use sesame seeds). Season with salt and pepper.

9 Scatter the bread crumb mixture (alternatively, just scatter the sesame seeds) over the top and bake until those are deeply and thoroughly crispy and golden brown, 8 to 10 minutes.

10 Remove from the oven and let cool slightly before serving.

DO AHEAD Gratin (sans bread crumbs) can be baked 2 days ahead, then kept covered and refrigerated. To reheat, place in a 400°F oven, uncovered (adding bread crumbs, if using), until returned to its bubbling, golden state, 10 to 15 minutes.

Beets with Buttermilk and Walnuts

serves 4 to 8

1½ pounds medium golden or
    red beets, scrubbed and tops
    trimmed
¼ cup red wine vinegar, white wine
    vinegar, or distilled white vinegar
Kosher salt
½ small red onion, thinly sliced
2 tablespoons fresh lemon juice,
    plus more to season
Freshly ground black pepper
½ teaspoon ground sumac (optional)
½ cup buttermilk (see page 14)
¼ cup sour cream or full-fat Greek
    yogurt
½ cup coarsely chopped walnuts,
    pecans, or hazelnuts, toasted
    (see page 14)
1 tablespoon cumin seeds, finely
    chopped or crushed
Olive oil, for drizzling

EAT WITH
Perfect Herby Salad (page 86)
+
Yogurt-Marinated Leg of Lamb with
Spicy Fennel and Sumac (page 204)

Peeling a freshly roasted beet is one of those therapeutic kitchen tasks I truly enjoy, like shelling peas and picking the stems off green beans. It's even more therapeutic when they're golden beets rather than red, so I don't stain my clothes, hands, kitchen towels, and countertops, but I still enjoy the task, regardless. Because of their intense sweet, earthy flavor, for me to really love a beet I have to eat it with something very creamy, very tangy, and very herby. Luckily, this dish has all of that, plus nutty crunchiness from some toasted walnuts (although you can use another nut, if you like) and cumin seeds.

1 Preheat the oven to 425°F.

2 Place the beets in a large baking dish and pour the vinegar over. Season with salt and cover the baking dish with foil. Roast until the beets are totally tender and can easily be pierced with a fork, 50 to 60 minutes. Let cool.

3 Combine the onion and lemon juice; season with salt and pepper. Let sit a minute or two, then add sumac, if using.

4 Meanwhile, combine the buttermilk and sour cream; season with salt, pepper, and some lemon juice.

5 Spoon the buttermilk mixture on the bottom of a large shallow bowl or sloped serving platter. Peel and slice the beets about ½ inch thick. Arrange them on top of the buttermilk mixture, then top with the onions, walnuts, and cumin. Drizzle everything with olive oil before serving.

DO AHEAD Beets can be roasted and peeled a few days ahead, covered tightly, and refrigerated. Buttermilk mixture can be made a week ahead, covered, and refrigerated.

Long-Roasted Eggplant with Garlic, Labne, and Tiny Chile Croutons

serves 4 to 6

3 medium or 2 large globe or Italian
  eggplants (about 2½ pounds),
  halved lengthwise
¾ cup olive oil, divided, plus more
  as needed
Kosher salt and freshly ground black
  pepper
2 garlic cloves, thinly sliced
1 fresh red chile, very thinly sliced,
  or 1 teaspoon crushed red pepper
  flakes
2 cups torn bread (crusty bread
  such as sourdough, country loaf,
  or miche), in ½-inch pieces
1 cup labne, full-fat Greek yogurt, or
  sour cream
1 preserved lemon, finely chopped
1 tablespoon fresh lemon juice, plus
  more as desired
1 cup fresh mint or cilantro leaves,
  tender leaves and stems

EAT WITH
Black Lentils with Crispy Garlic and
Labne (page 167)
+
Citrusy Cucumbers with Red Onion
and Toasted Sesame (page 96)

Eggplant is a truly special vegetable (okay, it's a fruit) with special powers. The texture, depending on how it's cooked, can be crispy, tender, or creamy, not unlike a potato. But unlike a potato, it also has the potential to be downright custardy. I'm talking, "Is this a flan? Are there eggs in this? Am I eating chawanmushi?" custardy. I don't want to make the other vegetables jealous, but I'm not sure there is anything else out there that can do what eggplant does.

Here, that custardy texture is impossibly easy to achieve when the eggplant gets halved lengthwise, drenched in olive oil, and roasted at a very high temperature. It never quite crisps, but it browns. Boy, does it brown. It browns and caramelizes while the rest of it turns to the texture that reminds me of the inside of a perfectly just set 6-minute egg. A true miracle.

So why add the labne, an already very creamy ingredient? Well, even once roasted in a glut of olive oil, eggplant is quite lean, so it takes kindly to those rich, fatty ingredients such as labne, yogurt, sour cream, cheese, and the like. All that is to say: Trust me. Since crunch is my favorite flavor, I like to scatter the whole thing with lots of olive-oily, garlicky fried spicy croutons.

This can absolutely fly as a fantastic main course for vegetarians or whoever just doesn't feel like eating meat at the moment. If you're going that route, just make sure there's at least one large half of an eggplant per person.

1 Preheat the oven to 425°F.

2 Using a small paring knife, make a few ½-inch slits into the cut side of each eggplant. (You can do this lengthwise, crosswise, or even diagonally. Knock yourself out with your decorative prowess!)

3 Place the eggplant cut side up on a rimmed baking sheet and drizzle with ½ cup olive oil, distributing as evenly as possible. Season with salt and pepper and turn over so that the eggplant is cut side down.

4 Place in the oven and roast, without moving or disturbing, until eggplant is completely tender, cooked through, and golden brown on the bottom (since the skin is already so dark, it can be hard to tell, but the skin will look shriveled and, when poked, the whole thing should feel tender, on the verge of collapse; you can also use a spatula to lift up the eggplant to check the underside for color), 40 to 45 minutes.

5 Meanwhile, heat the remaining ¼ cup olive oil in a large skillet over medium heat. Add the garlic and chile and cook, shaking the skillet occasionally, until the garlic and chile are frizzled and fragrant (but not yet browned), 1 or 2 minutes. Add the bread and season with salt and pepper. Cook, stirring frequently, until the bread is evenly toasted and golden brown, 3 to 5 minutes. Remove from the heat and set aside.

6 Combine the labne, preserved lemon, and 1 tablespoon lemon juice in a small bowl; season with salt, pepper, and more lemon juice, if you like. Smear it onto the bottom of a large serving platter or in a shallow bowl.

7 Once the eggplant is good and ready to go, use a fish spatula (or regular spatula) to lift up each eggplant half in one fell swoop, preserving its lovely golden underside. Place the eggplant, cut side up, on top of the seasoned labne. Scatter with the crispy croutons and herbs before serving.

DO AHEAD Eggplant can be roasted a few hours ahead, then kept loosely covered at room temperature (no need to reheat— it's excellent at room temperature). The labne can be seasoned a week ahead, covered tightly, and refrigerated. The croutons can be made 2 days ahead and kept covered tightly at room temperature.

Garlicky Broccoli and Greens with Hazelnut and Coriander

serves 4 to 6

2 garlic cloves, finely grated

½ cup toasted hazelnuts, finely chopped

1 tablespoon coriander seeds, finely chopped

¼ cup plus 3 tablespoons olive oil, divided, plus more for drizzling

Kosher salt and freshly ground black pepper

2–3 large heads of broccoli, quartered lengthwise, about 1½ pounds

1 large or 2 small bunches lacinato or curly kale

1 lemon, halved crosswise

Flaky sea salt

If you haven't had grilled broccoli, dare I say "You haven't lived"? The stalk, which is painfully underused, is so insanely good when charred over actual flames that you may never eat it any other way. (Unless you're blanching it, as on page 139. What can I say? Either light it on fire or dunk it in boiling water, I live in a world of extremes.) This is probably one of the best vegetable dishes to eat at room temperature, so if you're stressed about getting everything ready at the same time, make this dish and feel relaxed knowing it will only get better as it sits.

1 Combine the garlic, hazelnuts, coriander seeds, and 3 tablespoons olive oil in a large bowl. Season with salt and pepper and set aside.

2 Heat a grill on high (alternatively, preheat the oven to 450°F).

3 Toss the broccoli and kale on a rimmed baking sheet with the remaining ¼ cup olive oil and season with salt and pepper. Grill, turning or tossing occasionally, until the stalks, florets, and leaves are lightly charred, anywhere from 2 to 8 minutes on the grill. (Alternatively, roast on a rimmed baking sheet until lightly charred and crisped, 15 to 20 minutes.)

4 Whether you're grilling or roasting, once the broccoli and greens are charred and tender (the leaves and stalks will cook at different rates, so keep an eye on them), add them to the bowl with the garlic and hazelnuts, tossing to coat.

5 Once all the goods are in there, transfer the ingredients to a large serving plate, platter, or bowl. Top with a good squeeze of lemon, a sprinkle of flaky salt, and a drizzle of olive oil.

DO AHEAD Broccoli and kale can be cooked and dressed a few hours ahead, then kept loosely covered and stored at room temperature.

The Greatest Creamed Greens

serves 4 to 6

¾ cup freshly made coarse bread crumbs (see page 14) or panko (optional)

2 tablespoons olive oil, plus more if using bread crumbs

Kosher salt and freshly ground black pepper

1 cup heavy cream

4 garlic cloves, peeled and smashed

⅛ teaspoon freshly grated nutmeg

2 large bunches kale, mustard greens, spinach, broccoli rabe, or swiss chard, thick stems removed, coarsely chopped (about 16 cups total)

½ cup crème fraîche

My love for creamed greens is directly related to my love for old-school steakhouses, which is deep and unwavering. There, the creamed greens are often so rich and decadent you can hardly eat more than a spoonful, but at my steakhouse (which is my regular house), the wilted greens are tossed with just enough simmered cream to count as creamed, so luckily, you can eat the whole thing.

1 If using bread crumbs, toss them in a small bowl with 3 tablespoons of olive oil and season with salt and pepper. Toast them in a large skillet over medium–high heat, tossing frequently until they're well toasted and crisped, 3 to 5 minutes. Remove from the heat and set aside.

2 Bring the cream to a simmer in a medium pot over medium heat. Add the garlic and nutmeg and season with salt and pepper. Simmer until reduced by about half, 15 to 20 minutes; it should be thick and very, very rich (it'll dilute a bit once you add it to the greens).

3 Heat 2 tablespoons olive oil in a large Dutch oven over medium heat. Add the greens, a handful at a time, and season with salt and pepper. Cook, adding more greens when the ones in the skillet wilt down. Stir frequently, until all the greens are bright green and the water starts to evaporate, 5 to 8 minutes, depending on the type of greens. Continue to cook until most of the water has evaporated and they're totally tender, another 5 minutes or so.

4 Add the cream mixture and crème fraîche, season with salt and pepper, and mix to evenly coat everything in the thick, creamy business. Cook a minute or two to make sure everything is hot before transferring to a bowl. Scatter with the bread crumbs, if using, and serve.

DO AHEAD Creamed greens can be made a few hours in advance, stored loosely covered at room temperature. Rewarm over medium heat before topping with the bread crumbs.

Crispy Vinegared Potatoes with Dried Chile

serves 4 to 6

**2 pounds Yukon Gold potatoes,
scrubbed and sliced about ¼ inch
thick (better they are too thin
than too thick)**
¼ cup distilled white vinegar
¼ cup olive oil
**1 teaspoon crushed red pepper
flakes**
1 teaspoon smoked paprika
**Kosher salt and freshly ground black
pepper**
1 small garlic clove, finely chopped
**¼ cup finely chopped fresh parsley,
tender leaves and stems, or
chives**

I'm always looking for ways to get the effect of something deep-fried (crispy, oily, salty) without having to bring bottles of oil to a terrifyingly high temperature in my own home. I mean, it really just seems too dangerous. That said, roasted potatoes, by all accounts, are almost always just "fine," but rarely transcendent. Too much soft interior, not enough crispiness, and I want *all* crispiness.

I find these potatoes are a good example of "having it all." Magically, they have the texture of something fried without having to be fried. They taste like a salt and vinegar chip without having to open and then eat an entire bag of salt and vinegar chips. Thinly sliced into rounds, they are doused in distilled white vinegar (for tanginess) and olive oil (for crispiness) with a judicious dusting of paprika for heat, color, and *je ne sais quoi*, roasted and transformed to slightly chewy, mostly crispy, salty, oily potatoes.

1 Preheat the oven to 425°F.

2 Combine the potatoes, vinegar, oil, crushed red pepper flakes, and paprika on a rimmed baking sheet. Season with salt and pepper and toss to coat.

3 Roast, tossing occasionally, until deeply golden brown and starting to crisp, just like a potato chip, 20 to 25 minutes.

4 Meanwhile, combine the garlic and parsley in a small bowl; season with salt and pepper.

5 Let the potatoes cool a little bit. (Resist the urge to eat one straight from the oven: it will burn your mouth, and while I'd like to say they are worth it, nothing is, okay?) Then, sprinkle with the parsley mixture and serve with literally anything.

DO AHEAD These potatoes should not really be done ahead, as they are best served right out of the oven. You can absolutely do the parsley-garlic mixture in advance; just know that chopped garlic intensifies once cut, so be prepared.

Farro with Toasted Fennel, Lemon, and Basil

serves 4 to 6

2 cups pearled or semi-pearled
    farro, barley, Israeli couscous,
    freekeh, or wheat berries
¼ cup olive oil
6 garlic cloves, thinly sliced
1 tablespoon fennel seeds
1 large fennel bulb, bulb stem thinly
    sliced, fronds reserved
1 lemon, thinly sliced, seeds
    removed
Kosher salt and freshly ground
    black pepper
Pinch of crushed red pepper flakes
    (optional)
1 cup fresh basil leaves, torn

NOTE *Since this grain salad
is so accommodating, feel free
to make it your own by adding
more herbs (basil! tarragon!),
a grating of salty cheese
(ricotta salata or pecorino),
or handful of toasted and
chopped nuts for texture.*

This is a very good and very polite grain salad recipe, maybe my favorite one in this book. It is not offensive to any other dish on the table and it'll get along with any other vegetable or protein you're serving. It has interesting things to say but doesn't dominate the conversation, and even if you think you have everything you need for dinner, you're always happy to see it because it makes excellent leftovers. Am I taking this metaphor too far?

This can also be made with any grain you please (except maybe rice), because, wow, what a polite and accommodating grain salad! Okay, I'll stop. But seriously, after making this, with the triple fennel (caramelized fennel, toasted seeds, and fresh fronds), softened slivers of garlic, and my favorite ingredient—whole lemon—there's no way you won't be this excited, too.

1 Cook grains according to package instructions. Drain and set aside.

2 Heat the olive oil in a large skillet or pot over medium heat. Add the garlic and fennel seeds, and cook, stirring occasionally until garlic is just starting to brown, 3 to 4 minutes. Add the sliced fennel bulb and half the lemon and season with salt and pepper. Cook, stirring occasionally, until the fennel is totally tender and starting to caramelize, 8 to 10 minutes.

3 Add the farro to the skillet and season with salt, pepper, and a pinch of crushed red pepper flakes, if using. Toss to coat and cook a few minutes, letting the farro absorb some of that garlicky, fennel-y olive oil. Add remaining lemon slices and chopped fennel stem and remove from heat. Transfer to a serving platter or bowl and top with the basil and fennel fronds.

DO AHEAD Farro can be cooked up to 5 days ahead, covered, and refrigerated. The whole dish can be cooked 2 days ahead, but wait to add the fresh herbs and fennel fronds.

Black Lentils with Crispy Garlic and Labne

serves 4 to 8

2 cups black (beluga) or French
(Puy) lentils
Kosher salt
½ cup olive oil
6 garlic cloves, thinly sliced
1 large shallot, thinly sliced
Coarsely ground black pepper
1 cup labne, full-fat Greek yogurt, or
sour cream
2 tablespoons finely grated lemon
zest, plus ¼ cup fresh lemon
juice, divided
2 cups fresh cilantro or parsley,
tender leaves and stems, finely
chopped
Flaky sea salt

EAT WITH
Little Gems with Garlicky Lemon and
Pistachio (page 88)
+
Just-Cooked Cabbage with Butter,
Anchovy, and Lemon (page 143)
+
Low and Slow Rib Roast with Rosemary
and Anchovy (page 218)

For literally no reason other than that they look like little beads of caviar, I have convinced myself that black lentils are somehow the fanciest of all legumes. They appear expensive and complicated, but are actually pretty cheap and can be cooked just like pasta. But I love them the most for their unparalleled texture and resilience to mushiness. They are more grain-like in texture than, say, red lentils, which tend to fall apart at the suggestion of a simmer (great for things like stews and dals, but less so for this). If you can't find black lentils, French lentils are a good substitute.

These lentils are served kind of like a seven-layer nacho situation (not an accident!), so be sure to serve with a big serving spoon for scooping.

1 Cook the lentils in a large pot of boiling salted water until tender and cooked through (but not turned to mush), 20 to 25 minutes. Drain and set aside.

2 Meanwhile, combine the olive oil, garlic, and shallot in a medium skillet over medium heat. Cook, swirling occasionally, until the garlic and shallot are nicely browned and starting to crisp, 4 to 5 minutes. Remove from the heat and season with salt and pepper.

3 Combine the labne with 2 tablespoons lemon juice and season with salt and pepper.

4 Toss the lentils with the lemon zest and remaining 2 tablespoons lemon juice, and season with salt and pepper. Spoon half of the lentils into a serving bowl and top with the cilantro. Cover with remaining lentils. Dollop with the seasoned labne and spoon the garlic mixture over top. Sprinkle with flaky salt and pepper before serving.

DO AHEAD Lentils can be cooked up to 5 days ahead, wrapped, and refrigerated.

Frizzled Chickpeas and Onions with Feta and Oregano

serves 4 to 6

½ cup olive oil

1 large red or yellow onion, thinly
  sliced

Kosher salt and freshly ground black
  pepper

2 (15-ounce) cans chickpeas, drained
  and rinsed

4 garlic cloves, smashed

Pinch of crushed red pepper flakes

4 sprigs fresh marjoram or oregano,
  plus more leaves for garnish

2 ounces Greek, Bulgarian, or
  French feta, very thinly sliced
  or crumbled

EAT WITH
Vinegared Apples with Persimmon and
White Cheddar (page 103)
+
Slow-Roasted Oregano Chicken with
Buttered Tomatoes (page 189)

I'm not sure that "frizzled" is a technical term, but once you cook these onions with these chickpeas, you'll understand what I mean and realize that there is no other way to describe them. Not quite fried, not quite caramelized, they sizzle and crisp and caramelize in a good amount of olive oil along with smashed garlic, resulting in what can only be described as frizzled.

This is good once you stop there, but adding fresh marjoram and tangy feta makes this a truly dreamy dish that I have eaten as my main meal more than once, nuzzled up next to a very runny, crispy-edged fried egg.

1 Heat the olive oil in a large skillet over medium-high heat. Add the onion and season with salt and pepper. Cook, stirring occasionally, until the onion has softened, and is just starting to brown, 5 to 8 minutes.

2 Add the chickpeas, garlic, red pepper flakes, and half the marjoram leaves. Season with salt and pepper and toss to coat in the oily business. Continue to cook, shaking the skillet occasionally to make sure nothing is sticking and that the chickpeas are getting equal attention from the oil and heat, until the chickpeas are golden brown and appear fried around the edges and the onion is a deep golden brown and looks somewhere between fried and caramelized, a term we now call "frizzled."

3 Taste a chickpea or two and make sure it's plenty seasoned, adding salt, pepper, and/or a pinch of red pepper flakes, if you like things on the spicier side.

4 Remove from the heat and transfer to a large serving bowl. Top with the feta and remaining marjoram.

DO AHEAD Chickpeas can be made a few hours ahead, kept covered loosely at room temperature. Feel free to reheat in a skillet over medium-high heat before serving, as they'll lose a bit of their crispness as they sit.

a big pot of brothy beans

If there's an argument for shelling and cooking your own beans, it is the promise of a giant pot of brothy beans. I mean the fresh shell beans you see at farmers' markets and specialty grocers, and maybe have overlooked because they seem complicated or time-consuming. Well, they are one of those things (time-consuming), but luckily for me, shelling beans is among my top five favorite meditative tasks, next to hot yoga and peeling off a face mask. Aside from the excellent zone-out you'll get while you absentmindedly shell the beans and dream of an Italian vacation, there is something truly special about a freshly shelled and cooked bean that you will have to taste to understand. Tender yet firm, never mushy or starchy with a delicately vegetal flavor, they really are a different beast.

I'm sure it's possible, but I have never made less than what could be considered "a giant pot" of beans at a time. This is fine, because their uses are truly endless. Depending on the flavor profile you're after and what their final destination is, the list of things you can add to the pot is highly customizable, but the basic formula is beans + aromatics + water. If you're using fresh shelling beans, know that you'll lose a lot of weight in the shelling process so always overcompensate (i.e., 5 pounds of beans will only get you around 3 cups of beans). If using dried beans, use any type you like: white or black, spotted or freckled, brown or beige, large or small—just make sure they are not old.

TO MAKE (for 4 to 8 people)
In a large pot, place **2 to 3 cups fresh or dried beans** (about 5 pounds fresh or 1 pound dried). Start with an oniony or garlicky something (an **onion**, a few **leeks**, a couple heads of **garlic**), making sure to halve them lengthwise to expose their insides. Add a few sprigs of herbs (**thyme**, **marjoram**, **oregano**, or **rosemary**) and if you like it hot, some **crushed red pepper flakes** or whole, **dried chilies** (the smoky ones like chipotle are excellent for flavoring the cooking liquid).

Cover with enough water to submerge the beans by about 4 inches. Season with a good amount of **kosher salt** (maybe slightly less than what you'd do for pasta water) and bring to a simmer over medium-high heat. Reduce the heat to medium-low and let them very gently simmer uncovered until the beans are tender, creamy, and cooked through, 40 to 50 minutes for fresh beans, closer to 80 to 90 minutes for dried (add water as needed to keep them submerged).

Once the beans are cooked, remove from the heat and store them in their cooking liquid. Once drained, you can add to escarole salad (page 82), turn them into a spicy, tomato-y side dish (page 48), or even marinate 'em in vinegar and garlic for an excellent pre-dinner snack (page 56). Kept still in their brothy, beany liquid, they are amazing slightly crushed and served as an unfussy side, spooned over thick cut toast, or added to a pot alongside a very large piece of pork (page 209) to braise together.

Tomato-y Beans with Preserved Lemon and Bread Crumbs

serves 4 to 6

½ cup olive oil, divided, plus more
    for drizzling
1 cup coarse fresh bread crumbs
    (see page 14) or panko
Kosher salt and freshly ground black
    pepper
1 small white onion, thinly sliced
2 garlic cloves, crushed or thinly
    sliced
3 tablespoons tomato paste
2 chiles de arbol, or ¾ teaspoon
    crushed red pepper flakes
2 cups fresh or dried shell beans, or
    2 (15-ounce) cans white beans,
    drained and rinsed
½ preserved lemon, thinly sliced

NOTE *I do think you would
be pleased making these with
fresh or dried shell beans
(page 171), but I am a Virgo
and we are people-pleasers
and so there is, of course, an
option for making this with
canned beans (a pantry staple
I happen to love).*

I love treating my beans like pasta, adding a skilletful of garlicky, caramelized tomato sauce, finished with salty preserved lemon and topped with oily, crunchy bread crumbs. Because they are beans and not pasta, there is no need to worry about them overcooking in the sauce, so feel free to simmer until they are flavorful enough to serve, adding water as needed to keep them saucy.

1 Heat ¼ cup of the olive oil in a large heavy-bottomed pot over medium-high heat. Add the bread crumbs and season with salt and pepper. Cook, stirring occasionally, until the bread crumbs have become toasted and golden brown, 4 to 6 minutes. Transfer to a small bowl.

2 Wipe out the pot and heat the remaining ¼ cup olive oil over medium-high heat. Add the onion and garlic. Season with salt and pepper, and cook, stirring occasionally, until they're translucent and tender, 5 to 7 minutes. Add the tomato paste and chiles, and continue to cook until the tomato paste has turned a nice brick-reddish color, about 2 minutes.

3 Add the beans and 6 cups water if using shell beans (2 cups water if using canned), shaking the skillet to scrape up any bits that have caramelized on the bottom. Season with salt and pepper and cook until the beans have turned creamy and tender and most of the liquid has evaporated, 45 to 50 minutes for shell beans, 15 to 20 minutes for canned beans.

4 Add the preserved lemon, then transfer beans to a serving bowl and top with the bread crumbs, letting them settle into the juicy bits of the beans.

DO AHEAD Bread crumbs can be made a day ahead, kept wrapped tightly at room temperature. The beans can be made sans bread crumb topping up to 2 days ahead, stored wrapped and refrigerated. Rewarm over medium heat, adding a splash of water if needed to keep things saucy.

Buttered Turmeric Rice with Crushed Almonds and Herbs

serves 4 to 6

1½ cups jasmine, basmati, or
    Jasmati rice (see Note)

Kosher salt

6 tablespoons (¾ stick) unsalted
    butter

2 tablespoons olive oil

¾ cup whole raw almonds, finely
    chopped

2-inch knob of fresh turmeric,
    peeled and thinly sliced, or
    ½ teaspoon ground turmeric

1 large shallot, thinly sliced

Freshly ground black pepper

1 cup fresh cilantro, tender leaves
    and stems, coarsely chopped

½ cup fresh mint and/or dill, tender
    leaves and stems

NOTE *You can also use
3 cups of cooked rice (leftover
or otherwise).*

EAT WITH
Perfect Herby Salad (page 86)
+
Buttered Salmon with Red Onion
and Dill (page 247)

I've taken a negative public stance on rice in the past, and generally speaking, I stand by that stance. But people can grow—so let me say this: Rice, sometimes you are great. Through a brief sizzle in butter, you become impossibly toasty, crispy, and full of flavor, which I have accused you of lacking in the past. While other grains like barley or farro would also work here, you are the best thing for this particular dish.

Inspired by classic Tahdig (crispy Persian rice), this version full of fresh herbs and buttery, toasted almonds more or less gets the job done, without requiring the patience or technique (I have neither!).

1 Cook the rice in a pot of salted boiling water until just al dente, 10 to 12 minutes. Drain, rinse, and set aside.

2 Heat the butter and olive oil in a large cast-iron or nonstick skillet over medium heat. Add the almonds and cook, stirring, until fragrant and toasted and the butter has started to brown, 3 to 4 minutes. Transfer the almonds to a small bowl, leaving all the butter behind, and season with salt.

3 Add the turmeric and shallot to the skillet and season with salt and pepper. Cook, stirring occasionally, until the shallot has softened but is not yet browned, 2 to 3 minutes. Add the rice and, using a spatula or wooden spoon, press the rice gently into the skillet, encouraging even contact all over. Cook, without disturbing the rice (feel free to rotate the skillet to prevent uneven cooking), until it's starting to brown nicely along the bottom (this will happen faster at the center of the skillet, so use a spatula to lift up the rice to check the progress), 8 to 10 minutes. Transfer to a large serving platter, placing some of those crispier bits of rice on top, along with the cilantro, mint, dill, and almonds.

DO AHEAD The plain rice can be cooked up to 5 days ahead, covered tightly, and refrigerated. The buttered rice can be made an hour ahead, kept in the skillet and covered loosely.

Lemony White Beans and Escarole with Anchovy and Parmesan

serves 4 to 6

¼ cup olive oil

4 garlic cloves, thinly sliced

4 anchovy fillets

2 tablespoons salted capers, rinsed, or 1 tablespoon brined

1 teaspoon crushed red pepper flakes

2 (15-ounce) cans white beans, such as cannellini, great northern, or navy, drained and rinsed

Kosher salt and freshly ground black pepper

1 head of escarole or chard, trimmed and torn into large pieces, divided

½ cup fresh mint leaves

½ cup fresh parsley leaves, tender leaves and stems

A hunk of parmesan or pecorino cheese, for serving

1 lemon, halved

These white beans could potentially be a whole meal themselves, especially if you're looking for a meatless main kind of deal, but I also love them solo alongside another protein because they're really pulling double duty as part starch, part salad—great for when you want both but don't feel like making both. While this dish is beautifully seasonally agnostic, I do dream about eating it with a grilled whole trout (page 244) or lamb shoulder with garlicky tomatoes (page 206) and lots of cold red or white wine, preferably in the summery, sunny outdoors, even if that just means my stoop, since I do not have a backyard.

1 Heat the olive oil in a large skillet over medium heat and add the garlic. Cook, swirling the skillet occasionally until the garlic is pale golden brown, 3 to 4 minutes.

2 Add the anchovies, capers, and crushed red pepper flakes, swirling until the anchovies melt and sizzle, the capers pop slightly, and the red pepper flakes toast and bleed into the oil, about 2 minutes.

3 Add the beans and season with salt and pepper. Reduce the heat to medium-low and toss to coat the beans in all the garlicky business. Let them cook until the flavors have melded and beans no longer taste like they came from a can, 8 to 10 minutes.

4 Add half the escarole and toss to coat, letting it wilt ever so slightly. Transfer the beans and wilted escarole to a large serving platter or bowl, and mix in the remaining escarole. Scatter with the mint and parsley. Use a peeler or box grater to shave some parmesan over all. Squeeze the lemon over everything just before serving.

DO AHEAD This side dish is really best prepared right before it's going to be eaten—if you must do it ahead, you can do everything up until step 3 a day before. When it's time to eat, reheat the beans and continue with step 4.

Tiny Creamy Pasta with Black Pepper and Pecorino

serves 4 to 6

4 tablespoons (½ stick) unsalted butter

2 tablespoons olive oil, plus more for drizzling

6 garlic cloves, thinly sliced

3 cups fregola, Israeli couscous, ditalini, or other small pasta (about 1 pound)

Kosher salt and freshly ground black pepper

5–7 cups water

1 cup finely grated pecorino or parmesan cheese, plus more for sprinkling

2 tablespoons finely chopped chives, for garnish

4–6 large egg yolks (optional)

EAT WITH

Iceberg with Pecorino, Crushed Olives, and Pickled Chile (page 91)
+
Spicy Pork Meatballs in Brothy Tomatoes and Toasted Fennel (page 187)

This very Americanized, not-at-all-authentic, sort-of riff on *cacio e pepe*–risotto hybrid is not much to look at, unless you like to look at a pot of white creamy starch—but holy hell, is it delicious! The egg yolks are optional, but they add that much more creaminess. I would serve this alongside any vegetables to offset the starchy cheese you're about to eat, but none would go better than aggressively lemony steamed broccoli (page 139).

1 Melt the butter and oil in a large pot over medium heat. Add the garlic and cook until lightly toasted, 2 to 3 minutes. Add the fregola and season with salt and pepper. Cook, stirring occasionally, until the pasta is well toasted, 2 to 3 minutes.

2 Add 5 cups of water and bring to a boil. Reduce the heat to medium and continue to cook at a strong simmer, stirring frequently to encourage the releasing of the starch (almost like you're making a risotto) until the pasta is cooked through, the water is almost completely evaporated, leaving behind a creamy, starchy sauce, 20 to 25 minutes (add water as needed to keep it saucy while the pasta finishes cooking).

3 Add the pecorino and season again with salt and *lots* of black pepper. Continue to cook until the pasta has the texture of risotto or a porridge, a few minutes or so (and add a splash of water if needed to keep things saucy).

4 To serve, transfer the pasta mixture to a bowl and top with the chives and egg yolks, if using, plus more black pepper and more pecorino cheese. (Alternatively, spoon the creamy pasta into individual serving bowls and top each with an egg yolk, lots of pepper, and more pecorino.)

DO AHEAD Pasta can be made an hour or two ahead of time, kept covered and stored at room temperature. Reheat low and slow, adding a splash of water to loosen things up, as the pasta will absorb most of the liquid as it sits.

mains

Deciding what to serve as the main course is often the most stressful part of having people over.

To lessen this emotional burden, I often start by deciding what the main event is going to be ("main course" sounds so formal) and then figure out everything else from there. I'm not suggesting that you need to design a full-blown menu with pairings; choosing what to serve can be as simple as "I feel like a roast chicken," or as complicated as "I need something that can effortlessly feed 10 to 12 people and they don't eat beef and I definitely do not want chicken." (You should make a pork shoulder.)

By design, these mains are relatively fuss-free and easy to execute regardless of how many people are eating. Some take a few hours but are hands-off, some will come together in under a half an hour but will require your attention the whole time. They have bold yet flexible flavor profiles (and therefore they are easy to pair with any number of salads or sides) with tons of optional, casual serving suggestions to enhance or simplify your dinner. That said, everything in this section could be suitable for lunch or a very intense breakfast, so live your truth.

Butcher's Steak with Dried Chiles and Salted Peanuts

serves 4 to 6

FOR THE SALSA

¾ cup canola or grapeseed oil, plus more as needed

2 ounces dried New Mexican chiles, stems removed (see Note)

2 ounces dried Guajillo chiles, stems removed, cut into rings

4 garlic cloves, smashed

¼ cup dry-roasted peanuts or toasted hazelnuts

2 tablespoons apple cider vinegar or distilled white vinegar

Kosher salt

FOR THE STEAK

1½ pounds hangar steak, boneless short ribs, strip steak, or any other beef steak of your choosing

Kosher salt and freshly ground black pepper

½ small onion, thinly sliced

2 tablespoons canola oil

1 bunch watercress, stems trimmed

2 tablespoons fresh lime juice, plus 2 limes, quartered

1 bunch fresh cilantro, tender leaves and stems

8–16 corn tortillas, warmed

NOTE *If you can't find New Mexican chiles, do not substitute fresh, as they are a completely different beast. If you live in an area where they don't sell dried chiles at grocery stores, the internet is an excellent resource.*

This is not a recipe for tacos, but rather a prelude to tacos, inspired by the food in one of my favorite cities, Oaxaca. There, you're more likely to find large platters of charred, grilled meats served alongside (not in) fresh corn tortillas with herbs, vegetables, and tons of lime for a more DIY situation, a style of eating I actually enjoy more than assembled tacos. The tangy, smoky, peanutty salsa (a.k.a. salsa macha) is by no means authentic—just a recipe cobbled together from what I remember something tasting like in a place I love very much. If you can, go to Oaxaca and have the real deal. Hopefully, this is good enough to convince you to book a ticket.

1 Make the salsa. Heat the oil, chiles, and garlic in a small pot over medium heat. Cook, swirling occasionally, until the chiles are toasted and the garlic is golden brown, 4 to 6 minutes. Remove from the heat and add the peanuts, swirling to coat. Transfer the mixture to a blender or food processor and pulse until coarsely pureed. Place in a bowl with the vinegar and add more oil as needed to create a spoonable sauce. Season with salt.

2 Make the steak. Season the steak with salt and pepper; set aside. Place the onion in a bowl of ice water and let sit (this rinses away some of that raw onion-y bite).

3 In a large skillet, preferably cast-iron, heat the oil over medium-high heat. Add the steak and cook until deeply, impossibly, golden brown on one side, 4 to 6 minutes. Flip and continue to cook until golden brown on that side as well, another 4 to 6 minutes. Transfer to a cutting board to rest 5 to 10 minutes.

4 Toss the watercress with the lime juice; season with salt and pepper. Slice the steak and serve alongside the onions, watercress, cilantro, lime wedges, chile-peanut salsa, and tortillas.

DO AHEAD The salsa can be made up to 2 weeks ahead, covered, and stored in the refrigerator.

sausage party

A "Sausage Party" is, as I'm sure you guessed, a fun party wherein you serve many kinds of sausages alongside many interesting and wonderful condiments. This does not have to be an outdoor grilling event (I have seen successful winter sausage parties thrown indoors), although it lends itself very well to summer days when it's too hot to cook inside.

The Sausage Party doesn't have rules, but it does have guidelines. First, there can and should be a wide assortment of sausage-like things to cook or grill: bratwurst, knockwurst, chorizo, nitrate-free local organic sausages, and overly salty ballpark-style hot dogs. Aside from that, keep it to things that do not require utensils, like peppers or corn on the cob that can be grilled alongside. It should go without saying, but hamburgers are not and will never be invited to a Sausage Party.

On the bun beat, I would be remiss not to endorse my all-time favorite bun, the Martin's Potato Roll. But whatever your choice, the bun must be sturdy enough to get lightly grilled or toasted and then filled without falling apart. As for condiments, there should be more than you think you need. Sausage garnish is an extremely personal matter, and sensitivity to that should not be ignored. For example, if I were to attend a sausage party and there was no yellow mustard, I would have to leave and go buy yellow mustard so that I could enjoy myself.

Similarly, I would never, ever put ketchup on a sausage or hot dog, but I know some people for whom it is nonnegotiable, so I will always provide. Even if you don't like spicy brown mustard, you should probably have it on hand. Generally speaking, the condiments should be purchased, not only because excellent homemade ketchup is a lie we tell ourselves but because this party is supposed to make you feel relaxed and confident, not like you're scrambling to open a Stonewall Kitchen.

If you're itching for a more DIY vibe, here's a little secret: Many dips double as a condiment. I would especially recommend the Labne with Sizzled Scallions and Chile (page 22), which is basically ranch dressing, or maybe a Lemony Aioli (page 37), which is Brooklyn for "mayonnaise." This kind of party is also the perfect opportunity to try new things you are "condiment curious" about. Kimchi from the farmers' market, hot sauce made in the basement of your cousin's best friend, that crazy harissa paste you've been wanting to try. There should be many different types of pickles alongside hot pickled peppers, finely chopped raw onion, maybe a debut of your homemade sauerkraut—anything goes here. Just make sure you have plenty of tangy and spicy things for either eating snuggled alongside or atop the sausages or simply on the plate as an in-between snack.

Aside from the buns and chips (you must have both), there should be a few salady numbers, like a spicy red cabbage situation (page 99), crushed potatoes with celery (page 135), or a simple grain salad (page 164). Remember these are just suggestions. Every Sausage Party is a personal journey!

Spicy Pork Meatballs in Brothy Tomatoes and Toasted Fennel

serves 4 to 6

6 garlic cloves (2 grated, 4 thinly
   sliced)
½ cup finely chopped fresh chives
½ cup finely chopped fresh parsley,
   tender leaves and stems, plus
   more for garnish
½ cup full-fat Greek yogurt
2 teaspoons fennel seeds, plus more
   for garnish
2 teaspoons hot smoked paprika
1½ teaspoons kosher salt
1 teaspoon crushed red pepper
   flakes, plus more for serving
1½ pounds ground pork, lamb, beef,
   and/or turkey (feel free to mix!)
Freshly ground black pepper
2 tablespoons olive oil, plus more
   for drizzling
1 large shallot, thinly sliced
2 pints Sungold or cherry tomatoes
   (about 1½ pounds), halved
¼ cup distilled white vinegar or
   white wine vinegar
3 cups water
1 cup fresh mint leaves
Piece of pecorino or parmesan,
   for grating
Toast or crusty bread, for serving

Historically speaking, I have a bad attitude about meatballs. (I don't love ground meat, and also I once was dumped the morning after a meatball-forward meal, and, yes, I blame the meatballs.) But I will say that I am coming around. After all, meatballs are undeniably excellent for serving large amounts of people, and here we have crispy, garlicky pork in a delicious, garlicky, tomato-y sauce. What's not to love?

I will give you a heads-up here: While one is not better than the other, these are less red-sauce Italian and more Isle of Capri Italian (do they even have meatballs there? I'm not sure). They simmer in a light, brothy tomato sauce flecked with toasted spices and lots and lots of garlic, then are finished with fresh herbs, salty cheese, and an ocean of olive oil, if you're doing it right. Bound by yogurt with no bread crumbs or egg in sight, the meatballs are light, springy, and accidentally gluten-free, which is great—especially if you're gluten-free, I imagine.

But for me, what really sets these meatballs apart is that they go the fresh-tomato route rather than the canned-tomato route, which I suppose makes them more a late-summer meatball rather than a wintry meatball. If you can get Sungold tomatoes for this, they will light up your life and make this a pot of sunshine that you cannot help but dip some very toasty bread into, so as to not waste any of the delicious, porky sauciness (if not, cherry tomatoes will do the trick).

1 Place the grated garlic in a medium bowl along with the chives, parsley, yogurt, fennel seeds, paprika, salt, and crushed red pepper flakes. Mix until well combined.

2 Add the meat, season with pepper, and, using your hands, mix until well combined. Roll the mixture into balls about 1½ inches in diameter (about the size of a plum; I like these meatballs on the smaller side). Place on a baking sheet or large plate.

(recipe continues)

NOTE *These meatballs and their tomato-y broth really want something to dip in, like simple crusty bread, or perhaps very good garlic bread (page 73). They also want some bitter greens (like Escarole with Mustard and Spicy Guanciale Bread Crumbs, page 82), which can actually be eaten out of the same bowl, the leaves taking a brief dip in the broth to soften slightly—wow, yes please.*

3 Heat the olive oil in a large, heavy-bottomed Dutch oven over medium-high heat. Add a few meatballs at a time, taking care not to crowd the pot. Cook, using tongs or a spatula to occasionally gently rotate them, until they are all golden brown all over (they may not hold their perfectly round shape, but that is more than okay), 8 to 10 minutes. As the meatballs are browned, transfer them to a large serving platter or plate. Leave the remaining bits and fat in the pot.

4 Add the shallot and sliced garlic to the pot and season with salt and pepper. Cook, stirring occasionally, until the shallot is tender and the garlic starts to brown a bit, 2 to 3 minutes.

5 Add the tomatoes and season with salt and pepper. Cook, stirring occasionally, until they burst and start to become all saucy and caramelize a bit on the bottom of the pot, 5 to 8 minutes. Add the vinegar and water, scraping up any bits along the bottom. Bring to a strong simmer and reduce the sauce by about one-fourth, just until it thickens slightly (it should still be relatively brothy), 5 to 7 minutes.

6 Return the meatballs to the pot and reduce the heat to medium-low. Simmer until the meatballs are cooked through and the flavors have melded, 10 to 15 minutes.

7 Remove from the heat. To serve, top the meatballs (either in individual bowls or right in the pot) with the mint and more crushed red pepper flakes and fennel seeds, if you like. Drizzle with some olive oil and serve with the cheese for grating and some toast for dipping.

DO AHEAD The meatball mixture can be made up to 1 day ahead (either kept in a bowl or shaped into meatballs), wrapped, and refrigerated (or up to 1 month in the freezer). The whole dish can be made up to 2 days ahead, covered, and refrigerated.

Slow-Roasted Oregano Chicken with Buttered Tomatoes

serve 4 to 6

3½- to 4-pound chicken

Kosher salt and freshly ground black pepper

¼ cup olive oil

1½ tablespoons fennel seeds, crushed in a mortar and pestle or spice mill, or chopped with a knife

1 bunch fresh oregano

1½ pounds small-ish vine-ripened tomatoes (about 6), halved lengthwise

2 heads of garlic, halved crosswise (don't worry about leaving the skin on; it's fine)

2 tablespoons unsalted butter

2 tablespoons red wine vinegar or white wine vinegar

4–6 1-inch-thick slices of good country bread, such as country loaf or sourdough, toasted (optional)

NOTE *Get ready for an unpopular opinon. Crispy-skinned chicken is a myth and a lie. Even when remotely crispy out of the oven, it will soften and deflate the second you slice into it. At best, there may be crispy bits, but to think you can somehow get the skin of an entire chicken shatteringly crispy will only lead you to frustration and disappointment.*

There are about a million ways to roast a chicken, and someone will always tell you that theirs is the best way. Here is my truth: If you smear a good, high-quality chicken with enough fat, season it with plenty of salt, roast it until it is cooked through and the skin is brown, it will always be excellent. But if you ask me (and you've got the time), it's the slow roast that gives you everything you want: perfectly golden skin, extremely tender meat, and plenty of salty, savory chicken juices to serve as a sauce.

Above all other dishes in this book, this chicken truly embodies the "nothing fancy" mood. From the extremely simple assemblage of ingredients to the ridiculously hands-off preparation, it's casual in a way that feels almost lazy (but isn't), with "make sounds after you take a bite" levels of delicious. You could truly put things over the edge and add a few anchovies to the tomatoes. (Mandatory anchovies might make me seem like a one-trick-pony, but let's pretend I'm not!)

1 Preheat the oven to 325°F.

2 Season the chicken with salt and pepper (if you can do this in advance, please do; think of it as a casual brine). Drizzle it with the olive oil and sprinkle with the fennel seeds.

3 Stuff the cavity with half the oregano and place in a large baking dish. Scatter the tomatoes, garlic, butter, and remaining oregano around the chicken. Roast until the chicken is golden brown and completely cooked through, and the tomatoes are nice and jammy, 2½ to 3 hours. Add the vinegar to the tomatoes and let the chicken rest in the baking dish for 10 minutes.

4 Place toast on serving platter and spoon the jammy tomatoes over or around the toast. Carve the chicken and place on top of the toast to catch the juices.

DO AHEAD The chicken can be roasted a few hours ahead; it's very good at room temperature.

I love wine

There is no greater pleasure than a bottle of extremely drinkable grape juice that's been fermented to create alcohol, which makes you feel good and warm and like the most fun and relaxed version of yourself. What I'm trying to say is: I love wine. I love white wine, orange wine, pink wine, red wine. I love wine that's chilled and wine that's not. I love wine with bubbles and wine without.

So how to know what wine to pick? Well, wine distribution tends to be very regional, which means what you're able to find in California will be different than what you can find in Texas, so to give specific examples here isn't so useful. (Plus, although it might look like one, this is not a wine book and I am not a wine expert.) My advice is to start by asking for suggestions from people who know more than you about wine. This can be the person who runs your local wine shop, the server at your favorite restaurant, or your friend who won't shut up about "Pét-Nats."

Tell them what you're looking for, using as many specific context clues as possible. For example, some things I have asked for are "something that tastes like kombucha" or "a light red that is better cold than not." Another helpful thing is to take a picture of any bottles you know you like and show it to someone you're buying wine from. Even if they don't have the exact wine, they'll likely be able to point you in the right direction depending on what they know about the grape, where it's from, and how it's made.

Above all else: Do not be afraid to sound like you don't know what you're talking about: Most of us don't! I'd rather be honest and inquisitive (even if that reads as "ditzy") than end up with a bottle of wine I don't like.

Regarding pairings: I don't really believe in them—not at restaurants and especially not at home. I think the best wine to drink with whatever you're eating or cooking is whatever wine you enjoy drinking, period. White wine is great with red meat, and if you want a juicy Gamay with your whole fish, then I think that's just perfect.

TO STORE

You have to keep your wine the right temperature, which for me is usually IMPOSSIBLY COLD, especially for whites, roses, and anything with bubbles. I tend to chill most of the reds I'm drinking these days, but that is not a steadfast rule to apply to all red wine. My refrigerator is comically small, so when I entertain I end up storing wine (and other beverages) in a sink or tub filled with lots of ice. This keeps the fridge clear to hold everything else without having to get rid of favorite condiments. Plus, the beautiful dramatic presentation of storing wine in your sink or bathtub is *chef kisses fingertips*.

One-Pot Chicken with Dates and Caramelized Lemon

serves 4 to 6

3½- to 4-pound chicken, or
   3 pounds bone-in, skin-on
   chicken thighs or legs
Kosher salt and freshly ground black
   pepper
4 tablespoons olive oil, divided
1 lemon, cut into thick slices
   crosswise, seeds removed
2 shallots, halved lengthwise
4–6 medjool dates (3 ounces), pitted
4 sprigs fresh thyme or oregano,
   plus more for serving
1 cup water
2 teaspoons ground Urfa chile,
   or 1 teaspoon crushed red pepper
   flakes
Flaky sea salt

EAT WITH
Perfect Herby Salad (page 86)
+
Frizzled Chickpeas and Onions with
Feta and Oregano (page 168)

This one-pot oven-cooked chicken is a true treasure. It's sweet and tangy and a little spicy, and just downright special. It's got the kind of bold flavors you wouldn't expect from such few ingredients, which I guess is part of what makes it remarkable. But it's also a rather flexible dish, able to be made with a whole chicken or chicken parts (bone-in, skin-on thighs, if you please) for a more weeknight-friendly vibe. But what makes it *really* special is how it's cooked: first seared, breast side up, letting the legs and thighs brown and render, then lemons and shallots are fried in that fat, then water is added to provide adequate sauciness, cooking the chicken quickly yet gently. The lid is then removed so the top can finish browning. And then there you have, all at once, a chicken that is both nearly fall-apart tender and deeply golden brown on all sides. A chicken revelation!

1 Preheat the oven to 425°F.

2 Season the chicken all over with salt and pepper. Heat 2 tablespoons of the oil in a large (at least 8-quart) Dutch oven over medium-high heat. Place the chicken in the pot breast side up, and using tongs or your hands (be careful!), press lightly to make sure the skin comes into even contact with the pot bottom. This is your chance to brown the legs and render that excess fat! It's rarely offered in whole-chicken recipes, so take advantage. (If using parts, just sear the chicken skin side down.)

3 Cook, without moving, until the chicken is nice and browned, 5 to 8 minutes. Seriously, no peeking! Nothing exciting will happen before 5 minutes, I promise you.

4 Add the lemon slices and shallot, maneuvering the chicken however you need so that the slices come into contact with the bottom of the pot. Let everything sizzle in the chicken fat until lightly caramelized, about 2 minutes.

5 Add the dates, thyme, and water. Sprinkle the top of the chicken with the Urfa chile and place the lid on. Put the Dutch oven in the oven and roast until the dates are plump, the lemon is jammy, and the chicken is almost but not totally cooked through, 20 to 25 minutes (it will look mostly cooked through and a little anemic from getting covered with the lid).

6 Remove the lid and drizzle the chicken with the remaining 2 tablespoons oil and continue to cook until the liquid has reduced by half and the top of the chicken is an illustrious, glistening golden-brown, another 20 to 30 minutes (depending on if you're using parts or whole bird).

7 Let the chicken rest in the Dutch oven for 10 minutes, then transfer to a cutting board and carve. Serve along with the shallot, lemons, and dates, with some more thyme and flaky sea salt sprinkled over.

DO AHEAD This chicken can be made a few hours ahead, then kept in the Dutch oven at room temperature. If you wish to reheat it before serving, pop it back into the oven without a lid for 10 to 15 minutes or so.

Sticky Chili Chicken with Hot-and-Sour Pineapple

serves 6 to 8

4 pounds bone-in, skin-on chicken (legs, thighs, breasts, and/or wings all work)

Kosher salt and freshly ground black pepper

½ cup light brown sugar

½ cup unseasoned rice wine vinegar

½ cup sambal or other chili paste

¼ cup fish sauce

¼ cup fresh lime juice

2 teaspoons crushed red pepper flakes

2 garlic cloves, finely grated

½ pineapple, peeled and cored, cut into 1½-inch spears or wedges

½ shallot or 4 scallions, thinly sliced

1 cup fresh cilantro, tender leaves and stems, coarsely chopped

2 tablespoons toasted sesame seeds

EAT WITH

Celery Salad with Cilantro and Sesame (page 100)

+

A pot of rice

I don't love sweet with my savory food, but this dish is an exception. The sticky, caramelized bits of pineapple that get basted with spicy chicken fat as they roast together are a match made in sheet-pan dinner heaven. While the oven treatment here is fantastic, I'd be lying if I said this wouldn't also be spectacular on the grill either in pieces (as it is here) using 100 percent wings, or assembled into everyone's favorite six-letter word: kebabs (!!!), using boneless, skinless parts cut into 1½-inch pieces and skewered.

1 Season the chicken with salt and pepper and place in a large resealable plastic bag or large baking dish.

2 Combine the brown sugar, vinegar, sambal, fish sauce, lime juice, crushed red pepper flakes, and garlic in a medium bowl, whisking to dissolve the sugar. Pour over the chicken, massaging to make sure everything gets equal love. Seal the plastic bag or wrap the baking dish and let sit at least 30 minutes, refrigerated.

3 Preheat the oven to 425°F. Place the chicken and pineapple on a rimmed baking sheet (for easier clean-up, line with foil or parchment). Drizzle the remaining marinade over everything and place in oven.

4 Roast until the chicken is deeply browned, caramelized, and cooked through (if you have a pastry or BBQ brush, feel free to baste the chicken and pineapple periodically with the rendered chicken fat juices), 50 to 60 minutes. By this time, the pineapple will also be impossibly golden and juicy, giving up all the goods, which makes for a delicious, sticky sauce.

5 Remove from the oven and transfer to a serving platter, carving up the chicken and slicing the pineapple for easier serving, if you like. Scatter with the shallot, cilantro, and sesame before serving.

DO AHEAD Chicken can be marinated 24 hours in advance.

Coconut-Braised Chicken with Chickpeas and Lime

serves 4 to 6

3½–4 pounds bone-in, skin-on chicken, preferably a mix of breasts, legs, and thighs

Kosher salt and freshly ground black pepper

2 tablespoons canola oil

4 garlic cloves, thinly sliced

1 large yellow or red onion, thinly sliced, divided

2 tablespoons gochujang (Korean chili paste) or tomato paste

2 tablespoons grated fresh ginger

2 tablespoons finely grated fresh turmeric, or 1 teaspoon ground

1 tablespoon cumin or fennel seeds

1½ teaspoons crushed red pepper flakes

2 (14-ounce) cans full-fat coconut milk

3 cups low-sodium chicken broth

2 (15-ounce) cans chickpeas, drained and rinsed

2 teaspoons fish sauce (optional)

1 cup fresh cilantro, tender leaves and stems

¾ cup roasted peanuts, coarsely chopped (optional)

2 limes, quartered

This chicken stew is sort of having an identity crisis (Is it *khao soi* inspired? *Tikka masala* leaning? Wait—why is there Korean chili paste in this recipe?), but I can assure you it is very happy living its best life as whatever type of fusion cuisine this is. Before you ask, yes, this can be made in an Instant Pot, but even if that is your preferred method, I beg of you to make this "the old-fashioned way" at least once. The smell of it gently simmering on your stove just might be the best thing to happen to you all year.

1 Season the chicken with salt and pepper. Heat the oil in a large, heavy-bottomed pot over medium heat. Sear the chicken, skin side down, until the fat has started to render, and it's evenly browned, 8 to 10 minutes. Turn the chicken over to continue to brown on that side too, 8 to 10 minutes.

2 Transfer the chicken to a large plate. Add the garlic and three quarters of the onion to the pot; season with salt and pepper. Cook, stirring occasionally, until softened, about 5 minutes. Add the gochujang, ginger, turmeric, cumin, and red pepper flakes and cook until the mixture is caramelizing on the bottom of the pot, about 2 minutes, adjusting the heat as needed to prevent scorching. Add the coconut milk and chicken broth and bring to a simmer. Return the chicken to the pot and add the chickpeas, seasoning again with salt and pepper. Reduce the heat to low, and place the lid on the pot, and walk away for at least 45 minutes.

3 After about 45 minutes, remove the lid and continue to gently simmer, uncovered, until the chicken is, indeed, fall-off-the-bone tender and the liquid has thickened, looking all nice and stew-like, 20 to 25 minutes. Add the fish sauce, if using. Serve the stew alongside the remaining onion, cilantro, peanuts (if using), and lime for squeezing over.

DO AHEAD Stew can be made up to 2 days ahead, kept covered in the refrigerator. Gently rewarm before serving.

Chicken and Mushroom Skillet Pie
with Greens and Tarragon

serves 4 to 6

2½ pounds bone-in, skin-on chicken
    thighs or breasts
Kosher salt and freshly ground black
    pepper
1 tablespoon canola oil
4 garlic cloves, thinly sliced
2 leeks, white and light green parts,
    thinly sliced, or 1 yellow onion
1 pound fresh mushrooms, such
    as morels, matsutake, cremini,
    or a combination, cut into
    bite-sized pieces
4 tablespoons (½ stick) unsalted
    butter
¼ cup all-purpose flour, plus more
    for the work surface
3 cups low-sodium chicken broth or
    1 more cup if forgoing the cream
1 cup heavy cream or crème fraîche
    (optional)
4 cups fresh greens, such as kale,
    torn into bite-sized pieces
¼ cup fresh tarragon, chopped
¼ cup chopped fresh chives or
    parsley, tender leaves and stems
1 disc The Only Pie Crust (page 311)
    or 1 (14-ounce) package puff
    pastry (1 sheet), thawed
1 large egg, lightly beaten

When I was a kid growing up in Los Angeles, sometimes it would be too hot to be outside in the summertime and I'd spend hours reading *Seventeen* magazine and watching *The Adventures of Pete and Pete* on loop. My summertime snack of choice? Ice-cold watermelon. Just kidding, it was microwaved chicken pot pies, courtesy of the West Coast queen of chicken pot pies herself, Marie Callender. Not exactly summertime refreshment, but hey, it was Los Angeles in the '90s and the A/C came on full blast any time it got above 75°F.

Anyway, I live in New York now, where my apartment doesn't have central A/C and I would literally never be able to convince anybody to come over for chicken pot pie in the middle of August, but it is a very cozy and appropriate meal for a cold evening. Are chicken pot pies cool? Absolutely not. Are they delicious, good for a crowd, and largely underrated? Absolutely, yes. Save them for your most intimate group of friends, so you don't have to bother with plates—just go for it straight from the dish. Serve with a peppery, watercress salad (page 87), or any bowl of lightly dressed, lemony, leafy greens.

1 Season the chicken with salt and pepper.

2 Heat the oil in a large ovenproof skillet over medium-heat. Add the chicken, skin side down, and cook until the skin is deeply golden brown and crisped and most of the fat has rendered, 10 to 12 minutes. Using tongs, flip the chicken and continue to cook until browned and mostly cooked through, another 8 to 10 minutes—the chicken will continue to cook through later.

3 Transfer the chicken to a large plate to rest, leaving all the fat and golden bits behind while you build the rest of the pie.

4 Add the garlic and leeks to the skillet and season with salt and pepper. Cook, stirring occasionally, until leeks are bright green and tender, about 4 minutes.

5 Add the mushrooms and season with salt and pepper. Cook, stirring occasionally, until the mushrooms and leeks have started to brown, 8 to 10 minutes.

6 Add the butter and let it melt, then add the flour. Stir to coat the vegetables. Cook just long enough to take the raw floury edge off but without browning, 2 to 3 minutes. Add the chicken broth, stirring to scrape up any bits on the bottom that may have stuck. Bring to a simmer and season with salt and pepper. If using cream, add it now; if not, go ahead and add an additional 1 cup broth and season with salt and pepper.

7 Separate the chicken meat from the bones, discarding any skin and cartilage. Add the chicken, greens, tarragon, and chives to the skillet and stir to mix everything well.

8 Preheat the oven to 425°F.

9 Roll out the dough on a lightly floured surface to a roughly 12-inch circle, oval, rectangle, or square depending on your baking dish (whatever shape it is, you want the dough just slightly larger than your vessel). Alternatively roll the puff pastry on a lightly floured surface to the same dimensions. Place the dough atop the filling, letting some dough hang over.

10 Use a pastry brush to coat the top of the dough with the beaten egg. Using a sharp paring knife, make a few slits in the center of the dough to allow some steam to escape (this will properly thicken the filling, as well as keep the crust flaky and crisp). Bake until the pastry is deeply golden brown (think the color of a good croissant) and the filling is bubbling up, 45 to 55 minutes. Let cool slightly before serving.

DO AHEAD You can prepare the filling up to 2 days ahead; transfer to your baking dish before placing the crust on top and proceeding. You can also fill the baking dish, put the crust on top (without the egg wash), and refrigerate for up to 24 hours until you're ready to egg wash and bake. You can also build the whole pie and wrap it, unbaked, and freeze it for up to 1 month. (This makes an excellent gift.) To bake from frozen, increase the baking time by 20 minutes.

Yogurt-Marinated Leg of Lamb with Spicy Fennel and Sumac

serves 8 to 12

4½- to 5½-pound bone-in leg of lamb

Kosher salt and freshly ground black pepper

¼ cup fennel or cumin seeds, finely crushed, plus more for serving

2 cups full-fat Greek yogurt, plus more for serving

6 garlic cloves, finely grated

¼ cup fresh oregano leaves, coarsely chopped, plus more for serving

1 tablespoon crushed red pepper flakes, plus more for serving

¼ cup olive oil, plus more for drizzling

¼ cup plus 2 tablespoons fresh lemon juice (from about 3 lemons)

2 large fennel bulbs, thinly sliced, divided

2 cups fresh parsley, cilantro, and/or mint, tender leaves and stems

Ground sumac (optional)

EAT WITH
Vinegar-Marinated Butter Beans
(page 56)
+
Chicories with Preserved Lemon,
Yogurt, and Mint (page 85)

When it comes to cooking a leg of lamb, I have some good news and some bad news. The bad news is that I understand a whole leg of lamb is large and expensive and intimidating. But here's the good news: its massive size and protective cloak of delicious, delicious fat make it difficult to overcook or dry out, especially when done low and slow.

Since roasting can still feel scary (and I like you all a lot!), I've also included instructions for braising and I can assure you: Both ways are insanely good. Roasting will give you something medium-rare and sliceable; braising will give you something fall apart tender and shreddy. Either way, you can cook the whole thing hours (or days) ahead of time, slicing or shredding when people are ready to eat (I love to serve sliced lamb at room temperature or even cold, but for the braise, you'll want to gently rewarm in an oven before shredding to loosen up the fat).

1 Using a sharp paring knife, score the lamb about ½ inch deep every few inches or so—this is a really large cut of meat and we aren't trying to keep it intact or anything, but we still want to cook it on the bone. Making these incisions will help season the meat deeply and cook more evenly. It seems like a fancy technique, but I promise, you can't mess it up.

2 Season the lamb with salt and pepper (you'll need at least 1 teaspoon kosher salt per pound here) and sprinkle with the fennel seed, making sure to get everything into those incisions.

3 Whisk the yogurt, garlic, oregano, crushed red pepper flakes, olive oil, and ¼ cup lemon juice in a medium bowl. Season with salt and pepper. As if you were applying a mud mask, smear the yogurt all over the lamb, making sure to get into any and all nooks and crannies (not just for English muffins!). Let the meat sit, lightly covered with plastic wrap, at room temperature for at least 1 hour or up to 2 hours, or wrap tightly in plastic and keep in the refrigerator overnight.

4 Preheat the oven to 300°F.

5 Scatter half the fennel at the bottom of a large roasting pan, and season with salt and pepper. Without wiping off excess marinade, place the lamb on top of the vegetables (or simply in the roasting pan), fat side up. (If braising, add 2 cups of water to the bottom of the roasting pan and cover tightly with foil.)

6 Roast, without touching or moving or peeking, until the lamb registers 115 to 120°F when a thermometer is inserted about 2 inches deep into the thickest part of the leg (taking care not to touch the bone), 60 to 90 minutes. (If braising, continue cooking until the lamb is extremely tender and nearly falling apart, 3 to 3½ hours. Remove the foil.)

7 Increase the temperature to 450°F and continue to cook until the lamb has reached 120 to 125°F and is deeply golden brown all over with little bits of charred marinade, 20 to 25 minutes more. (If braising, this step is just to brown and crisp up the outside of the lamb.)

8 Remove from the oven and let rest a few minutes.

9 Once the lamb is cooked to your liking, carve the larger lobes off the bone and thinly slice. Or, for more dramatic albeit slightly messier presentation, thinly slice lamb directly off the bone in the style of a large country ham or prosciutto—this is my favorite way. (If braising, using two forks, simply shred the meat into large pieces.)

10 Combine the remaining sliced fennel bulb and 2 tablespoons lemon juice, and season with salt, pepper, and crushed red pepper flakes. Add herbs and toss to coat.

11 Place lamb on a large platter and scatter with the fennel mixture, sprinkling with extra fennel seed and sumac, if using. Drizzle with olive oil and flaky salt and serve alongside extra yogurt.

DO AHEAD Lamb can be marinated 24 hours ahead, loosely covered, and refrigerated. Lamb can be roasted or grilled a few hours ahead, loosely covered with foil, and left at room temperature.

Grilled Lamb Shoulder over Fresh Garlicky Tomatoes

serves 6 to 8

2–3 pounds boneless lamb shoulder
12 anchovy fillets, finely chopped
¼ cup olive oil, plus more if needed
Kosher salt and freshly ground black
    pepper
2 pounds very ripe tomatoes, sliced
    ¾ inch thick
4 green garlic stalks, thinly sliced, or
    2 garlic cloves, finely grated
2 tablespoons fresh lemon juice,
    white wine vinegar, or red wine
    vinegar
Flaky sea salt
Lemony Aioli (page 37), full-fat
    Greek yogurt, or labne (optional)
Salsa verde (optional)
Flatbreads or some other bread
    (optional)

NOTE *A casual white bean salad with escarole (page 175) would be so fun and very on trend for my Italian fantasy (as would those Wine-Roasted Artichokes on page 128). The aioli, salsa verde, and flatbreads are all optional, but I highly recommend at least one or all three, throwing the bread on the grill to warm up and catch a little char as the meat rests, to drag through the tomato-y, garlicky lamby juices.*

When I envision myself at age seventy-two, living in the Italian countryside and caring for a resplendent yet manageably sized garden, along with several cats, this is what I plan on eating every day for lunch, a lunch that is so late and long that it may as well be dinner, washed down with a glass of white wine so crisp I could wear it as a shirt.

That said, I often cook and eat my weight in some version of this dish, especially in the late summer, when it's nice enough to grill outside without sweating. This dish is impossibly easy to throw together, and lamb shoulder is a delightfully forgiving cut on the grill—zero experience required (but I have also included instructions for cooking this on the stovetop).

1 Using a knife, separate the lamb shoulder where it naturally wants to separate, into 3 or 4 smaller pieces (almost like a few lamb steaks)—this is to ensure even cooking on the grill.

2 Mix the anchovies and olive oil. Season the lamb with salt and pepper and smear with the anchovy mixture (do this at least 30 minutes in advance, uncovered and refrigerated).

3 Heat a grill to medium-high. (Or heat 2 tablespoons oil in a large cast iron over medium-high heat.)

4 Grill the meat over the hottest part of the grill, flipping frequently to make sure nothing burns. Grill until charred deeply and evenly, 5 to 8 minutes, depending on the thickness of the piece. (Or sear the pieces of lamb until golden brown on all sides, 3 to 5 minutes per side.) Transfer the lamb to a cutting board and let rest for 10 minutes.

5 Meanwhile, place the tomatoes on a large serving platter and season with salt and pepper. Scatter with the green garlic and lemon juice and set aside. Thinly slice the meat and place immediately atop the tomatoes, letting the juices mingle. Sprinkle with flaky salt and, if desired, serve with aioli, salsa verde, and/or flatbreads.

Harissa-Rubbed Pork Shoulder with White Beans and Chard

serves 6 to 10

4 pounds boneless pork shoulder
Kosher salt and freshly ground black
  pepper
½ cup harissa paste
¼ cup distilled white vinegar
3 tablespoons tomato paste
3 tablespoons light brown sugar
4 garlic cloves, finely grated
1½ cups water
2 (15-ounce) cans small white
  beans, such as cannellini or great
  northern, drained and rinsed
1 large bunch chard, stems removed,
  leaves torn into bite-sized pieces
1 preserved lemon, seeds removed,
  thinly sliced
1 cup cilantro, tender leaves
  and stems
1 lemon, halved

NOTE *Pork shoulder is cheap, available at basically every grocery store and impossibly delicious no matter what you do to it. It is almost always my go-to "I want to have people over and have no idea what to cook" meat, especially useful for when you're not sure how many people are coming or what they like to eat, because (a) it miraculously always feeds the exact number of people you need it to, (b) it's impossible to mess up, and (c) everybody loves pork shoulder.*

There is no pre-sear or any other preliminary steps here before slathering the pork with a garlicky harissa paste and popping it into an oven, which makes it especially foolproof, even if cooking large pieces of meat usually freaks you out. You could certainly stop after you've braised the shoulder, serving the spicy, tangy pan juices over roasted potatoes or a fluffy pile of couscous, but I love adding the beans and returning them to a significantly hotter oven to absorb the crazy flavorful pork fat, getting a little browned and crisped as the pork also browns and crisps and, yes, this is a cute little play on "pork and beans"—thanks for noticing!

1 Preheat the oven to 325°F.

2 Season the pork with salt and pepper and place in a large Dutch oven. Combine the harissa paste, vinegar, tomato paste, brown sugar, and garlic in a medium bowl. Smear the harissa mixture all over pork, getting into all nooks and crannies, and add the water. Place the lid on the pot and roast, until the pork is nearly falling-apart tender, 3 to 3½ hours.

3 Remove the lid, add the beans, and season with salt and pepper. Increase the oven temperature to 425°F and return the pot to the oven, uncovered. Roast until the beans have soaked up all the liquid and the top of the pork is deeply golden brown, 40 to 45 minutes.

4 Transfer the pork to a cutting board. Add the chard and preserved lemon to the beans and stir to wilt the leaves. Slice pork into ½-inch-thick slices (if it starts to shred, that's fine). Transfer the beans and greens to a large serving plate or shallow bowl and place the pork on top (alternatively, place pork on top of the beans in the pot and serve directly from there). Scatter with cilantro and serve the lemon alongside for squeezing over.

DO AHEAD This can be made up to 3 days ahead, sans chard, stored in its pot, and refrigerated. Reheat before adding chard.

Kimchi-Braised Pork with Sesame and Egg Yolk

serves 6 to 8

FOR THE STEW

2½–3 pounds baby back ribs,
  separated into 2-rib segments, or
  2 pounds boneless pork shoulder,
  cut into 2-inch pieces
Kosher salt and freshly ground black
  pepper
2 tablespoons vegetable oil
4 garlic cloves, finely chopped
2-inch piece fresh ginger, peeled
  and finely chopped
¼ cup gochujang (Korean chili
  paste)
2 (16-ounce) jars cabbage kimchi,
  coarsely chopped
1 bunch scallions, green and white
  parts, cut into 1-inch pieces
8 cups water

I am calling this a braise, but it is really a stew (an homage to the Korean Jjigae) in which meat is braised—but isn't that most stews? Anyway, yes, this is a spicy, funky, gingery *stew* in which you will *braise* large chunks of pork and then top them with fresh, crunchy vegetables and maybe eat with some soft tofu and perhaps a creamy, raw egg yolk. You could certainly use something like pork shoulder instead of ribs, but I love the ratio of fat to meat in a baby back rib (and the bones are fun!).

The stew is amazing on its own (and not for nothing, excellent for a hangover or a very bad cold), but as with most things in life (and this book), I am here for the toppings. It's a fun thing to set out a giant pot of this stuff with several of your cutest bowls filled with this and that, making for a festive DIY party.

1 Make the stew. Season the pork with salt and pepper. Heat the oil in a large pot over medium heat. Working in batches if needed, add the pork and cook until golden brown on all sides. (Time will vary depending if you're doing ribs or shoulder, but all in all, should take 15 to 20 minutes to brown the meat all over.)

2 Transfer the meat to a cutting board or large platter, leaving the drippings and fat in the pot (feel free to scrape out any obvious burned bits). Add the garlic and ginger and cook, stirring occasionally, until the garlic starts to brown, 2 to 3 minutes. Add the gochujang and cook just like you would tomato paste, until it's caramelized and turned a sort of brick-red color, another 2 minutes or so.

3 Add the kimchi, scallions, and water. Bring to a simmer and nestle the pork into the liquid, making sure it's all submerged. Cover the pot and reduce the heat to medium-low. Gently simmer until the pork is falling apart and completely tender, 2 to 2½ hours.

**2 watermelon radishes or 4 regular
    radishes, thinly sliced**
1 apple, thinly sliced
2 tablespoons rice wine vinegar
1 tablespoon toasted sesame oil
**Korean chili flakes or crushed red
    pepper flakes**
1 (12–16 ounce) package silken tofu
**4 scallions, green and white parts,
    thinly sliced**
¼ cup toasted sesame seeds
**4 cups watercress, tough stems
    removed**
6–8 large egg yolks

4 To serve, toss the radishes and apple with the vinegar, sesame oil, and chili flakes, and season with salt and pepper. Place the tofu in a medium bowl (I leave it whole so people can spoon out as much as they want) and top with a bit of scallion and sesame seeds.

5 Let people DIY their own bowls. For reference, my dream bowl involves spooning a bit of tofu into the bottom of a bowl then ladling the stew over. From there, I top it with a little radish/apple mixture, a few sprigs of watercress, a sprinkling of sesame seeds and scallions, and last but not least: an egg yolk. But please design your own bowl of dreams, even if that means simply enjoying the stew on its own, as is.

DO AHEAD Kimchi stew can be made up to 3 days ahead (you can keep it in the pot), covered, and refrigerated. Rewarm gently over medium heat to bring to a gentle simmer and heat all the way through.

Citrus Chicken Rested in Herbs

serves 4 to 6

½ cup fresh lime or lemon juice
  (from 4–6 lemons or limes),
  plus 1 lime or lemon, thinly sliced
½ cup fresh orange juice,
  plus 1 orange, thinly sliced, seeds
  removed
½ cup soy sauce
2 tablespoons canola oil, plus more
2 tablespoons yuzu kosho or sambal,
  or 1 jalapeño, finely chopped
2 garlic cloves, finely grated
Kosher salt and freshly ground black
  pepper
3½- to 4-pound chicken, halved
  lengthwise through the backbone
  (see Note, page 216), or bone-in,
  skin-on parts
½ cup fresh cilantro, tender leaves
  and stems, coarsely chopped
½ cup fresh parsley, tender leaves
  and stems, coarsely chopped
A few sprigs fresh rosemary, thyme,
  oregano, or marjoram (optional)

Grilling a chicken that's been marinated and basted in sweet, tangy citrus, a bit of salty soy sauce, and a good amount of funky, spicy something (like yuzu kosho, Japanese fermented chili paste) is simple and pleasant and gets along with everything—kind of like your favorite T-shirt that you wear over and over again, or your really nice neighbor who always brings packages in for you when you're out of town. It's just a really good chicken, and honestly, sometimes that's all you need.

Since this marinade is so agreeable and the technique so straightforward, it's an excellent opportunity to add vegetables to cook alongside the chicken, if you like. Pick something quick cooking, like sliced fennel, a bunch of scallions, quartered radishes, or fresh chiles.

While the default here is for roasting, I've also included instructions for grilling, since this particular marinade works extremely well with the deep, smoky, charred flavors that come from the grill. If grilling, feel free to add some additional cut citrus so that it can char alongside the chicken, perfect for squeezing over when serving.

1 To make the marinade, combine the lime juice, orange juice, soy sauce, oil, yuzu kosho, and garlic in a medium bowl and season with salt and pepper. Set about half aside for later, and add the rest of the marinade to a large bowl, resealable bag, or baking dish. Add the chicken, tossing to coat well. Let it sit in the marinade for a while (at least 30 minutes, but up to 24 hours, in the refrigerator).

2 Preheat the oven to 450°F. (Alternatively, heat a grill to medium heat, with cooler coals or low flames on one side. You can grill the chicken over hotter flames, but it can be challenging to manage; for beginners, it's good to err on the side of the coals being slightly cooler than slightly hotter.)

(recipe continues)

HOW TO HALVE A CHICKEN

Not quite spatchcocking, you're literally just cutting the chicken in half lengthwise to create two equal halves. This is done to eliminate the air space in the cavity of the bird, which means it'll cook much faster. A cleaver is truly the best tool for this job, but who has a cleaver? Use the sharpest, heaviest knife you have.

Place the chicken on a cutting board breast side up and take your knife, splitting it directly in between each breast and pressing firmly with the knife until you reach the backbone, then keep going until you reach the cutting board. That's it! Two halves of one chicken.

3 Remove the chicken from the marinade (discarding the marinade the chicken was sitting in) and place skin side up on a rimmed baking sheet. Roast until the skin is deeply browned and lightly charred and the chicken is cooked through, 35 to 45 minutes; no need to flip or turn the chicken. (Alternatively, place the chicken skin side down on the grill and cover; make sure the vents are open. Let it grill, resisting the urge to turn or check too frequently, until it's nicely golden brown with those cute little grill marks, 10 to 12 minutes; just like when you're searing chicken in a skillet, the skin will release effortlessly once it's cooked and golden. Attempting to move it beforehand will probably tear the skin and maybe ruin your day! Using your finest and largest tongs, carefully flip the chicken and cover so that it continues to grill and cook on the other side, another 10 to 12 minutes. Flip once more, skin side down, and add a few halves of cut citrus. Continue to grill another 5 to 8 minutes, to recrisp the skin and finish cooking through.)

4 Place the remaining citrus slices on a platter or cutting board and scatter with the herbs. Place the cooked chicken on top, skin side up, and pour the reserved marinade over. Let the chicken rest for 10 to 20 minutes, allowing its juices to mingle with the fresh citrus and herbs. Carve the chicken into pieces before serving.

DO AHEAD Chicken can be cooked a few hours ahead, loosely covered with foil, and kept at room temperature. Serve either at room temperature or throw it back into a 450°F oven (or on the grill) for a quick reheat.

when things don't go well

I hope this book doesn't give you the impression that every time I have people over things go according to plan. Not only do they rarely go "according to plan," but honestly, there is rarely a plan to begin with. Not saying that's the best way to go about things, but it is how I live my life. So if you are the kind of person who does plan, then congratulations because you are already one step ahead of me.

In the event that things don't go well (Too many people show up and there's not enough food! Someone turns off the stove in the middle of braising your brisket and it now takes longer than you thought it would!), then there are always back-up plans, including: Ordering a few pizzas. Turning your seated dinner party into a standing dinner party. Embracing the chaos and laughing and trying to have a good time anyway. Life and cooking are not an exact science (I mean, technically, cooking is, but you get what I'm saying). To invite people into your home, to be a cook, you must possess some sort of flexibility. I struggle with this idea on a daily basis (my expectation vs. my reality), but accepting that things won't always go how I want them to when having people over is essential to enjoying what this is all about, anyway—having people over. So my advice to anyone asking for tips on how to deal with all this: be kind to yourself, manage expectations, and remember that this is supposed to be fun.

Low and Slow Rib Roast with Rosemary and Anchovy

serves 8 to 12

7- to 7½-pound whole bone-in rib roast (about a 3-bone roast), not frenched

Kosher salt and freshly ground black pepper

6 sprigs fresh rosemary

1 tin or jar of anchovy fillets (about 10 anchovies), plus more for serving (optional)

8 garlic cloves, finely grated

¼ cup olive oil

1 tablespoon canola oil

Flaky sea salt

1 cup fresh parsley, tender leaves and stems, finely chopped, plus more for serving

NOTE *Save these bones! Either separate them and eat as-is, crisp them in the oven, or use to make broth.*

EAT WITH
Shrimp Cocktail (page 36)
+
DIY Martini Bar (page 63)
+
Little Gems with Garlicky Lemon and Pistachio (page 88)
+
Baked Potato Bar (page 147)
+
The Greatest Creamed Greens (page 162)

Here is a great dinner party trick: Invite some people over for dinner. Don't stress out about all the things you're going to make; instead, focus all your emotional and financial efforts on one, glorious thing. Say it's a very large piece of slightly fancy red meat. Season it aggressively, love it passionately, and cook it perfectly at a low and gentle temperature. Do all of this before anyone gets there. Perhaps throw a few russet potatoes into a very hot oven to bake while you wait for everyone to arrive, because they'll only set you back about $4 and baked potatoes are amazing (see page 146). Throw together a very quick salad of maybe just some spicy leaves and a handful of herbs, but don't dress it with lemon just yet. Watch everyone file in and fill your home with the wine they brought. Pour yourself a glass! You deserve it.

When you're ready, take the baked potatoes out of the oven, ask someone to prepare some fixings for said potatoes (like opening a tub of sour cream). Finish your perfectly cooked meat by browning it in a skillet (or that very hot oven). Don't even bother to let it rest, because it doesn't need to (thank you, "Reverse Sear!" For more on that, see sidebar, page 221). Carve your insanely impressive piece of meat (be sure everyone sees you doing this), and then, last, dress your salad. Eat all these things together and feel happy that you did something nice for people you love by preparing them a fancy cut of meat in your own home, where the only price of admission was a bottle of wine. And the dishes—they have to do the dishes.

1 Season the meat with salt and pepper (you want 1 teaspoon of kosher salt per pound). Place on a rimmed baking sheet (preferably lined with a wire rack so that the meat does not sit directly in the liquid that escapes from salting, and let sit at least 2 hours at room temperature or up to 48 hours refrigerated.

(recipe continues)

2 Meanwhile, finely chop 2 sprigs of rosemary and about 10 anchovies and combine in a medium bowl with the garlic and olive oil. Season with salt and pepper.

3 Preheat the oven to 250°F.

4 Scatter the remaining 4 sprigs of rosemary on the bottom of a rimmed baking sheet. Smear the meat with the anchovy mixture and place on top of the rosemary. Place the whole thing in the oven and let it roast low and slow until a meat thermometer reaches 110°F (for medium-rare) when inserted into the deepest part of the meat, 2 to 2½ hours. Remove from the oven (the temperature will continue to rise as it sits—you're looking for an eventual 125°F temperature). Let it hang out for up to 4 hours at room temperature.

5 When you're ready to eat, heat the canola oil in a large cast-iron skillet over medium-high heat. Once the oil is smoking, add the meat, fat side down. Cook, pressing lightly to encourage the whole underside to make contact with the skillet, until it's deeply browned, 5 to 8 minutes. Flip the roast so that it's fat side up and remove from heat. (Alternatively, increase the temperature to 500°F, or however high your oven goes, and cook the roast until the fat is browned, 10 to 15 minutes—this is easier, but your fat will never get as browned and you'll miss out on pan drippings.)

6 Transfer the meat to a cutting board, leaving any juices behind in the pan.

7 Slice the roast away from the bones (see Note, page 218). Slice the roast however you please; I like mine on the thinner side, about ¼ inch slices, but some prefer thinner (like roast beef) or thicker (like prime rib). Place the slices on a large serving platter and pour over any juices left behind. Sprinkle with flaky salt and parsley, serving with more anchovies alongside, if you like.

DO AHEAD Roast can and should be seasoned up to 48 hours in advance. It can be roasted 3 hours ahead, then left loosely covered with foil at room temperature, just like they do at all the best prime rib restaurants.

the reverse sear

Here's a little pep talk if you're considering any seemingly intimidating recipe involving a large cut of meat (rib roast, page 218, or lamb, page 206): Do not be nervous, for the Reverse Sear is here to help. What's a reverse sear, you ask? Instead of taking a piece of meat and searing it, then transferring it to the oven to finish cooking, you start by cooking it low and slow in the oven, and once it's achieved the perfect internal temperature (125°F. for medium-rare), you sear it on the stovetop (or brown in an aggressively hot oven), then slice and serve. No resting, no worrying, no outer ring of well-done meat. I was skeptical of this cooking technique myself, wondering if it really was better or just new—until I tried it and became convinced that it was, indeed, the easiest and most foolproof way to cook a large-format cut of meat. Here's why:

1 Think of the time in the oven as additional seasoning time. Whatever you're rubbing the meat with (be it simply salt and pepper or the delicious garlicky anchovy mixture from page 218) has even more time to marinate.

2 As the meat roasts low and slow, the fat begins to render, which makes crisping up the meat at the end much easier and quicker. Doing it low and slow also means that there is no need to let the meat rest, since it's essentially, well, kind of "resting" the whole time.

3 Perhaps most convincingly, owing to the massive size of meat and extremely low roasting temperature, it's almost impossible to overcook (in fact, there is a higher likelihood of undercooking than overcooking, which is good because you can always pop it into the oven if it's too rare for you).

Spiced and Braised Short Ribs with Creamy Potatoes

serves 4 to 6

5 pounds bone-in short ribs,
  1½–2 inches thick
Kosher salt and freshly ground black
  pepper
2 tablespoons canola or
  vegetable oil
1½ pounds Yukon Gold potatoes
  (about 4), quartered lengthwise
2 small yellow onions, quartered
6 garlic cloves, thinly sliced
4 whole chiles de arbol, or
  1 teaspoon crushed red pepper
  flakes, plus more for serving
2 tablespoons cumin seeds
2 tablespoons fennel seeds
1 tablespoon coriander seeds
½ teaspoon ground cinnamon
2 tablespoons tomato paste
½ cup white wine vinegar
3 cups beef or chicken broth,
  or water
1 lemon, seeds removed, finely
  chopped

EAT WITH
Celery and Fennel with Walnuts and
Blue Cheese (page 95)
+
Bread for dipping
+
A very light, chilled red wine

Short ribs are an excellent cut if you love to be cozy and/or have an extreme fear of cooking red meat. Their outrageous marbling and fat content make them one of the easiest cuts to prepare and hardest to mess up. While I mostly see them done in an Italian way, all red wine-y and canned tomato-y, I prefer to take them in a spiced and citrusy direction to counter the intensity that is, well, a giant hunk of braised red meat.

The last step of the recipe is to uncover the perfectly tender and adequately cooked short ribs to crisp up the meat and potatoes and further thicken and reduce the sauce. It increases the cooking time by about 30-ish minutes, but it'll be the best 30-ish minutes you'll ever spend, I promise.

1 Season the short ribs with salt and lots of pepper. If you can do this the day before, even better (just store them uncovered and refrigerated).

2 Preheat the oven to 325°F.

3 Heat the oil in a large (at least 8-quart) Dutch oven over medium heat. Working in batches, sear the short ribs until deeply golden brown all on all sides, 12 to 15 minutes. Using tongs, transfer the short ribs to a large serving platter or rimmed baking sheet.

4 Carefully (the pot is hot!) drain excess fat from the pot, leaving behind about 2 tablespoons of fat and any of the good bits. Add the potatoes, cut side down, and season with salt and pepper. Cook, without disturbing, until they're nicely browned on one side, about 5 minutes. Give them a stir and continue to cook until browned a little more evenly. Using a slotted spoon, transfer the potatoes to the tray with the meat, leaving any bits and fat behind.

5 Add the onion and garlic to the pot and season with salt and pepper. Cook, stirring occasionally, until the onions have a nice golden brown color, 5 to 8 minutes. Add the 4 whole chiles, cumin seeds, fennel seeds, coriander seeds, and cinnamon, stirring to coat and toast the spices.

6 Add the tomato paste and cook, stirring constantly, until it's started to caramelize on the bottom of the pot (adjust the heat as needed to make sure it doesn't burn before it caramelizes), about 2 minutes. Add the vinegar, broth, and half the lemon and bring to a simmer, scraping up all the bits on the bottom of the pot.

7 Return the short ribs and potatoes to the pot, nestling everything in (if it's a tight squeeze, just make sure the short ribs get priority seating on the braise train, which is to say make sure they are submerged even if the potatoes are not). Cover and place the pot in the oven to roast until the short ribs are falling-off-the-bone tender and the potatoes are impossibly creamy to the point of almost mush (but not yet mush), 2½ to 3 hours.

8 Increase the oven temperature to 425°F and remove the lid. Continue to cook until the short ribs and any potatoes on top are browned and starting to crisp, and the liquid has reduced to a very nice, rich sauce, 25 to 35 minutes.

9 Scatter the meat and potatoes with the remaining lemon, plus a bit of crumbled chile before serving.

DO AHEAD Short ribs can be braised up to 2 days ahead, kept in the pot they were made in, covered, and refrigerated. Rewarm them covered, either gently on the stovetop over medium heat or in a 400°F oven, until they are warmed through and saucy.

Soy-Braised Brisket with Caramelized Honey and Garlic

serves 6 to 10

3½- to 4-pound boneless beef
    brisket, fat trimmed
Kosher salt and freshly ground black
    pepper
2 tablespoons canola oil
⅓ cup honey
2 heads of garlic, halved crosswise
    to expose the cloves (you can
    leave the paper on—it's okay)
2 large yellow onions, quartered
1 cinnamon stick
3 star anise pods
3-inch piece of fresh ginger, peeled
    and sliced
4 chiles de arbol, or ½ teaspoon
    crushed red pepper flakes,
    plus more
2 dried or fresh bay leaves
4 cups beef or chicken broth
1¼ cups low-sodium soy sauce
½ cup rice wine vinegar
2 tablespoons fish sauce
4 cups fresh cilantro, mint, and/or
    basil, tender leaves and stems
¼ cup thinly sliced chives or
    scallions
Cooked rice noodles or plain rice,
    for serving (optional)

Not to sound like too delicate a flower, but I tend to find most braised meat, especially beef, a little much for my liking. Too savory, too sweet, too heavy, too—just too much. As a general rule, I don't order it in restaurants, but the exception is the tangy, spiced braised beef noodles available at a few of my favorite Chinese restaurants around New York, which I'll order nearly every time. While not a replication, this brisket is my interpretation: salty from soy sauce, sour from vinegar, lightly spiced from a few pantry all-stars. I love cooking large cuts in a super-flavorful liquid low and slow enough till it's impossibly tender but not falling apart, so that it can be sliced rather than shredded, almost like a smoked brisket from a barbeque spot. Served over springy noodles with its brothy cooking liquid ladled over, scattered with an absurd amount of mixed herbs (it's a salad!), and not only is it not too much but also it's really never enough.

1 Season the brisket with salt and pepper. Do this as far ahead as possible (somewhere between 5 minutes and 48 hours is great).

2 Heat the oil in a large, heavy-bottomed Dutch oven (make sure it's got a fitted lid) over medium-high heat. Add the brisket, fattiest side down (if there is not a clear winner, any side will do) and sear, occasionally pressing with tongs to ensure even contact with the pot, until it's deeply golden brown, 8 to 10 minutes. Flip the brisket and sear on the other side until similarly, deeply, golden brown. Sometimes a brisket will have a third (or even fourth) side, depending on the shape and cut, so sear on all sides if applicable.

3 Transfer the brisket to a plate or platter and drain the pot of any residual fat into a heatproof container (no need to wipe it out). Return the pot to medium-high heat and add the

(recipe continues)

honey. Let it sizzle and bubble and start to caramelize, about 2 minutes. (If the pot is dark and you can't see it, don't worry, you'll smell it. It will smell like a rich, deep caramel.)

4 Reduce the heat to medium-low and add the garlic, onion, cinnamon, star anise, ginger, chiles, and bay leaves. Stir to coat in the caramelized honey and cook until they take on some color and soften a bit, 2 to 3 minutes.

5 Add the beef broth, soy sauce, vinegar, and fish sauce. Return the brisket to the pot, nestling it in there. If the brisket is not at least three-fourths covered, add more broth or water until it is.

6 Bring the liquid to a simmer, reduce the heat to medium-low, and cover. Simmer gently, peeking only when you absolutely can't stand how good it smells and need to check on it to make sure it's not ready (it's not), until it's totally, completely, impossibly tender, 3 to 3½ hours.

7 Using tongs or two spatulas, remove the brisket and transfer to a cutting board, reserving the braising liquid. If you like, use a slotted spoon or strainer to remove and discard the vegetables and spices from the pot (this is unnecessary, but a nice touch if you don't want to fish them out later).

8 Slice the brisket and return it to the pot with the liquid (you can also shred it, if that is your preference).

9 Toss the herbs and chives together in a medium bowl. Season with salt and pepper.

10 Serve brisket out of the pot or inside a shallow bowl, ladling some of the braising liquid over. Top with herbs and maybe a pinch of red pepper flakes. Serve with additional braising liquid for spooning over or drinking, and with rice noodles or rice, if you like.

DO AHEAD Unsliced brisket can be made up to 5 days ahead, stored in its liquid (you can keep it in the pot), covered, and refrigerated. Rewarm gently over medium heat to bring to a gentle simmer and heat all the way through.

lamb chops for the table

I am obsessed with the concept of a food "for the table." You may be wondering, *Isn't any food on the table . . . for the table?* Yes, sure, but this is more than that. Food "for the table" is a lifestyle choice. For example, at restaurants, when you can't commit to a whole pancake or waffle, encourage the table to order a "table pancake," a.k.a. "a pancake for the table," so that nobody is deprived or overcommitted.

Similarly at home, when I've planned on roasting a chicken or serving lasagna at dinner but then find myself unable to resist the most perfect little lamb chops at the butcher, I'll grab a few, take them home, season them simply, then sear and serve them in an extremely casual way. I always mention that it's not meant as the main event but, rather, a little snack (for the table!). This makes it feel like a special treat—and who doesn't love a special treat? No utensils required; I encourage people to just pick up the chops and eat them right off the bone, like we are at Medieval Times.

You could do this with a few things, I suppose, but to me, there is no better food "for the table" than individual crispy lamb chops. Serve them with A Very Good Lasagna (page 256), next to a summery seafood pasta (see page 250), or even with whole fish (see page 244) for an extremely spectacular surf-and-turf vibe. (Yes, that Green Goddess Butter, page 124, would be really great with lamb chops.)

To do this, you'll want to plan on 1 or 2 standard (not frenched) **lamb chops** per person. Ideally, they should be about ¾ inch thick, but this will vary. Seasoning them simply with **salt and pepper**, you're going to sear them in a large super-hot cast-iron skillet over medium-high heat until they're golden brown on both sides (4 to 6 minutes total). Once all the lamb chops you desire are cooked to crispy perfection, remove from the heat and add a good knob of **butter**, swirling to melt and sizzle, along with a few cloves of **smashed garlic** and a couple of sprigs of **fresh herbs** like **thyme** or **savory**. Transfer the lamb chops to a large serving platter, rimmed baking sheet, whatever you can find. Pour the butter/garlic/herb mixture over the lamb chops as they rest, finishing with a squeeze of **lemon** and a sprinkle of **flaky salt**. Deliver them to the table, indicating to whomever you're serving these chops to that it's really more of a snack and that they should feel empowered to take as many or as few as they like, making sure to cry out, "Lamb chops for the table!"

Grilled Shrimp with Crushed Fresh Tomatoes and Lots of Lime

serves 4 to 6

2 extremely ripe, large-ish tomatoes

2 garlic cloves, finely grated

4 tablespoons olive oil, divided, plus more for drizzling

Kosher salt and freshly ground black pepper

2 tablespoons fresh lime juice, plus more limes for serving

2½ pounds medium head-on shrimp (or prawns)

2 tablespoons unsalted butter

Pinch of crushed red pepper flakes or a few dashes of hot sauce (optional)

½ cup tender leaves and stems of fresh parsley or cilantro, coarsely chopped

Tortillas, rice, or toast for serving

EAT WITH

Tiny Peppers with Yuzu Kosho (page 64)

+

Charred Corn and Scallions with Tomatillo (page 113)

Despite my mild shellfish allergy, I love cooking and eating large amounts of crabs, lobster, crawfish or shrimp. There is a focused, ritualistic and possibly even hedonistic approach to the whole thing. Start by ripping off the head, maybe sucking the juices, then tearing the little limbs away, peeling back the shell (or sometimes eating it) to get at the very delicious, sweet meat. While you can do this with any aforementioned shellfish, every which way (grilled, steamed, boiled, sautéed), here, it's shrimp, and they're grilled (or sautéed, if you like). As they come off the heat, shells still hot, they're tossed in a bowlful of garlicky, crushed, preferably overripe tomatoes that have been further acidulated with lots and lots of lime and finished with a knob of butter. They're tossed repeatedly, encouraging the shrimpy juices to spill out so everything can get to know each other, creating a sauce that dreams are made of.

1 Using your hands, crush the tomatoes in a large bowl, breaking up any large bits. Add the garlic, 2 tablespoons olive oil, and salt and pepper.

2 Heat a charcoal or gas grill to high (alternatively, heat 2 tablespoons oil in a large skillet over medium-high heat).

3 Toss the shrimp with the remaining 2 tablespoons oil and season with salt and pepper.

4 Place the shrimp on the grill (or in a skillet), turning only once, until lightly charred and just cooked through, 3 to 4 minutes total, depending on size. Immediately transfer to the bowl with the crushed tomatoes and butter and toss to coat. Add crushed red pepper flakes, if using. Add the lime juice and let sit a minute or two; the heat from the shrimp will melt the butter, gently cooking the tomato and garlic.

5 Transfer the shrimp to a large serving platter or bowl, making sure to pour the tomato-y juices over everything. Top with the parsley, serving more limes alongside with warmed tortillas, a bowl of rice, or slabs of toast for mopping up juices.

Pan-Fried Sardines with Fried and Salted Lemons

serves 4 to 8

2 lemons, thinly sliced, seeds removed, divided

1 teaspoon ground sumac (optional)

Kosher salt and freshly ground black pepper

2 pounds whole fresh sardines, gutted and cleaned (they do not need to be scaled)

3 tablespoons olive oil, divided, plus more for drizzling

4 tablespoons (½ stick) unsalted butter

1 cup fresh parsley or cilantro, tender leaves and stems

Flaky sea salt

NOTE *There are people who would gladly sit down to a whole plate of sardines and only sardines, but most people need a little coaxing. For these people, I'd plan on 1 to 2 sardines per person, making sure you're supplementing the meal with something else like a pot of fennel-y, brothy meatballs (page 187), or a pot of pasta (page 253).*

Sardines get such a bad reputation for being fishy and fatty, but that's exactly why I love them. It's true, they are a fantastically oily, fatty, meaty fish, which means they are delicious! But it also means their quality deteriorates almost immediately once they leave the sea. That said, it is increasingly easy to find high-quality sardines, and when you see them, you should buy them and cook them. Preferably in lots of browned butter (fat + fat is always good) and tangy lemon (to cut through all that fat!), but don't let me tell you how to live your life.

1 Combine half the lemon slices and the sumac, if using, in a small bowl; season aggressively with salt and pepper—the lemons should be rather salty.

2 Season the sardines with salt and pepper. Heat 2 tablespoons of the olive oil in a large skillet. Working in batches, add a few sardines—as many as will fit without being packed like . . . sardines in a can (sorry!). Using a fish spatula, press each sardine lightly into the pan to encourage even contact. After 3 to 4 minutes, flip them and cook on the other side, another 3 to 4 minutes. The skin should look browned and lightly crisped, the meat inside opaque and cooked through (they are hard to overcook, so when in doubt, it's better to cook them a little longer). Transfer to a paper towel–lined plate or platter and set aside.

3 Wipe out the skillet, but don't worry about it getting it super clean. Return it to medium-high heat, then add the butter and let it foam and sizzle up, browning a bit in the skillet. Add the remaining 1 tablespoon olive oil and the remaining lemon slices, and season with salt and pepper.

4 Cook until the lemon slices are browned and lightly fried, about 4 minutes, then remove from the heat. Arrange the sardines on a large serving platter and pour the browned butter and fried lemons over, followed by the salted lemon slices, the parsley, a sprinkling of flaky salt, and a drizzle of olive oil.

Scallops with Spicy Beans, Tomatillo, and Citrus

serves 4 to 6

4 tomatillos, husked, rinsed, and thinly sliced

2 tangerines or small oranges, peeled, thinly sliced, seeds removed

1 small fresh green or red chile, thinly sliced, seeds removed for less heat if you like

1 small shallot, thinly sliced

2 tablespoons fresh lime juice, plus more for seasoning

6 tablespoons olive oil, divided, plus more for drizzling

Kosher salt and freshly ground black pepper

1½–2 pounds sea scallops, side muscles removed

2 tablespoons canola oil

1 (15-ounce) can cannellini or navy beans, drained and rinsed

2 teaspoons Aleppo-style pepper or 1 teaspoon crushed red pepper flakes

½ cup fresh cilantro, tender leaves and stems

Scallops (pronounced "SCAL-op" not "SKOL-op") are expensive, so when I cook them I prefer to sweeten the deal with something affordable that also makes them even more fun to eat. For me, "a can of beans" is truly my idea of "fun," especially when tossed in the skillet the scallops were seared in, soaking up all those crazy delicious, salty sticky scallop bits, then spooned over thick slices of citrus and crunchy, tangy tomatillos (which, if you haven't eaten raw, you're in for a treat).

I think of this dish as a sort of one-skillet meal (it's got protein and starch), but if you want, you could certainly serve it with tortillas or rice on the side.

1 Combine the tomatillos, tangerines, chile, shallot, lime juice, and 4 tablespoons olive oil in a large bowl; season with salt and pepper and set aside.

2 Season the scallops with salt and pepper. Heat the canola oil in a large skillet, preferably cast-iron, over medium-high heat. Working in batches, add the scallops and, using a fish spatula, press lightly to make good contact with the skillet. Sear until deeply browned, about 3 minutes per side.

3 Transfer the scallops to a large plate or serving platter. Without wiping the skillet, add the remaining 2 tablespoons olive oil, followed by the beans and Aleppo-style pepper, and season with salt and pepper. Cook, shaking the skillet occasionally, until the beans have soaked up all that scallop-y business and are looking impossibly tasty, about 4 minutes or so.

4 Transfer the tomatillos and citrus to a large serving platter and top with the beans, scallops, and cilantro. Drizzle everything with a little more olive oil before serving.

DO AHEAD Citrus and tomatillos can be cut a few hours ahead.

Halibut with Asparagus and Brown-Buttered Peas

serves 4 to 8

1½–2 pounds skinless halibut,
    salmon, arctic char, or other
    large, fatty firm fillet
1 bunch asparagus, the thinner the
    better, halved lengthwise if thick,
    tough ends trimmed
1 bunch spring onions, scallions,
    or ramps (!), halved lengthwise
    if thick
¼ cup olive oil, plus more as needed
Kosher salt and freshly ground black
    pepper
4 tablespoons (½ stick) unsalted
    butter, plus more if you want to
    live a little
2 cups shelled English peas (frozen
    are fine, too)
2 tablespoons finely chopped fresh
    chives, plus more for serving
2 tablespoons fresh tarragon leaves,
    finely chopped, plus more for
    serving
1 lemon, cut into wedges

EAT WITH
Lemony Aioli (page 37)
+
Wine-Roasted Artichokes (page 128)

I support the idea that ingredients that are difficult or expensive to farm, grow, source, fish, raise, and process should be, well, expensive. Good things are not cheap, and they shouldn't be. It's for this reason that I don't eat halibut very often, but when I do, I'm mentally and emotionally prepared to pay for it.

It's also for this reason that when I have a special ingredient (e.g., a large piece of gorgeous halibut, extremely in-season tomatoes, a perfect peach), I do just about nothing to it. If I'm paying half a month's rent for a piece of something, I want to taste that thing, not fourteen other ingredients. So yes, this is a simple fish dish cooked simply. Salt, pepper, and lemon—excellent fish needs nothing more.

1 Preheat the oven to 425°F.

2 Place the fish on a rimmed baking sheet and scatter the asparagus and spring onions around. Drizzle everything with olive oil and season with salt and pepper. Place in the oven and bake until fish is just cooked through, the ends of the spring onions have started to sizzle and crisp, and the asparagus can be easily pierced with a fork, 10 to 12 minutes.

3 Meanwhile, heat the butter in a medium pot over medium heat. Cook, swirling the pot occasionally, until the butter has started to brown and foam up, about 3 minutes. Use a spoon or small whisk to scrape up the browned bits on the bottom. Add the peas and season with salt and an aggressive amount of pepper. Add the chives and tarragon. Transfer to a medium bowl and top with more butter, if you like.

4 Serve the fish and vegetables, along with the lemon wedges for squeezing over, with the peas. Scatter everything with more tarragon, chives, and pepper, if you like.

Salmon with Soy and Citrusy Charred Scallions

serves 4 to 8

2 bunches scallions or spring onions, white and green parts, trimmed

2–3 pounds skin-on salmon fillet

¼ cup plus 3 tablespoons olive oil, divided

Kosher salt and freshly ground black pepper

¼ cup low-sodium soy sauce

1 tablespoon finely grated lemon or lime zest plus ¼ cup fresh lemon or lime juice (from about 2 lemons or 4 limes)

2 tablespoons fresh orange juice (from about 1 orange)

Crushed red pepper flakes

EAT WITH

Smashed Cucumbers with Sizzled Turmeric and Garlic (page 107)

+

A side of salmon roe

+

A bowl of rice

I used to be "not that into salmon" because my experience had only involved well-done salmon. You know the kind: firm, dry, flaky, and so pale you can barely tell it's pink. Then I discovered the slow roast, the oil poach, and the only-grill-on-one-side techniques, all of which yield an extremely tender, almost creamy textured salmon whose color is an actual representation of the name itself. That is the salmon that has made me a person who not just tolerates the fish but craves and makes it for herself. What a world!

This particular salmon is slow roasted until just cooked through, then doused in a citrusy, soy sauce-y, oniony mixture that is part sauce, part dressing. From there, you can do whatever you want, but I love the idea of serving it with a giant bowl of warm rice and salmon roe (salmon with salmon eggs is *so good*).

1 Preheat the oven to 325°F. Thinly slice 4 scallions and place in a medium bowl; set aside.

2 Place the salmon skin side down in a large baking dish and drizzle with 2 tablespoons olive oil and season with salt and lots of pepper. Place in the oven and roast until the center begins to turn from deep sunset orange to salmon-y pink, but still remains pretty medium-rare toward the top, 10 to 12 minutes.

3 Meanwhile, heat 1 tablespoon of the olive oil over medium-high heat in a medium cast-iron skillet. Add the remaining scallions and season with salt and pepper. Cook, tossing occasionally, until deeply charred in spots, 4 to 6 minutes.

4 Transfer the scallions to a cutting board and coarsely chop. Add to the bowl with raw scallions along with the soy sauce, lemon zest and juice, orange juice, and remaining ¼ cup olive oil; season with salt, pepper, and crushed red pepper flakes.

5 Using a large spatula, transfer the salmon to a large serving platter, leaving any skin behind. Spoon a bit of the charred scallion mixture over, serving any extra alongside.

Clams and Cod in Heavy Cream with Tiny Potatoes and Celery

serves 6 to 8

4 pounds manila clams or very small
   littleneck clams, scrubbed well
¼ cup olive oil, plus more for the
   bread
6 garlic cloves, thinly sliced
1 pound small waxy potatoes, sliced
   into ¼-inch-thick coins
Kosher salt and freshly ground black
   pepper
6 celery stalks, thinly sliced on the
   bias, plus leaves for garnish
½ teaspoon crushed red pepper
   flakes, plus more to taste
½ cup very dry white wine, such as
   Sauvignon Blanc (see Note)
1½ cups heavy cream
12 ounces cod or pollack, cut into
   2-inch pieces
1 cup fresh parsley, tender leaves
   and stems
1 lemon, for zesting and juicing
Toast or crusty bread, for serving

NOTE *As always, don't use a wine you wouldn't drink, but it's important to note that here you want to avoid any wine that you'd interpret as "sweet" or "oaky." I'm sure you don't need me to tell you this, but please feel free to drink the rest of the bottle with the clams.*

This clam dish is not quite a chowder, but it is decidedly chowder in spirit. The clams (or cockles, if you can find them!) get steamed open in a white winey, cream broth alongside potatoes, celery, and a bit of toasted garlic. Cod is then added, lightly poaching in the broth, and the whole thing is topped with lemony herbs and served with crusty, preferably almost-burnt toast. I love this eaten straight from the pot, like a shellfish free-for-all, but if you prefer individual bowls, that's cool, too.

1 Place the clams in a large bowl and let them soak in very cold water while you prepare the broth.

2 Heat the olive oil in a large pot (better if it's wider than tall) over medium-high heat and add the garlic and potatoes. Season with salt and pepper and cook, stirring occasionally, until the potatoes are totally softened and tender, 8 to 10 minutes.

3 Add the celery and red pepper flakes and season with salt and pepper. Add the wine and cook 2 to 3 minutes, until reduced by about half. Add the cream and bring to a simmer.

4 Add the clams, making sure they are nestled in there (but they don't all have to be submerged) and place the lid on top. Cook, resisting the urge to check for at least 5 minutes (a watched clam never opens). Once the clams start to open (4 to 8 minutes), give them a stir, encouraging the rest of them to open. If any clams are especially late to the party (so late they never open), remove and discard.

5 Add the cod, letting it nestle into the broth and season with salt and pepper. Place the lid on again and cook until the fish is cooked through, about 5 minutes. Remove from heat.

6 Toss the parsley and any celery leaves in a medium bowl. Juice and zest the lemon over and season with salt and pepper. Scatter over the pot before serving with toast or bread.

Swordfish with Crushed Olives and Oregano

serves 4 to 6

2 cups Castelvetrano olives (or similar mild green olive), pitted and crushed

2 tablespoons white wine vinegar or fresh lemon juice

Leaves from 6 sprigs fresh oregano or marjoram

¼ cup plus 2 tablespoons olive oil, divided

Kosher salt and freshly ground black pepper

3–4 swordfish steaks (8–10 ounces each), 1–1¼ inches thick

2 garlic cloves, thinly sliced

¼ cup fresh parsley leaves, tender leaves and stems

2 lemons, halved, for serving

EAT WITH
Lemony Watercress with Raw and Toasted Fennel (page 87)
+
Tomato-y Beans with Preserved Lemon and Bread Crumbs (page 172)

Swordfish is good for people who claim not to be into fish. Meaty and juicy, with little to no fishy flavor, it looks and kind of tastes like the best chicken breast you've ever had (really!). Especially so when you give it the kind of faux escabeche treatment, cooking the steaks to a delightful medium-rare, then dousing them in vinegary olives and onions to briefly marinate and firm up the meat. If the mood strikes and the weather cooperates, swordfish steaks are also excellent on the grill (either whole or cut into 1½-inch pieces and skewered on kebabs).

1 Combine the olives, vinegar, half the leaves from the oregano, and ¼ cup olive oil. Season with salt and pepper and let sit while you cook the swordfish.

2 Season the swordfish with salt and pepper. Heat the remaining 2 tablespoons olive oil in a very large skillet. Working in batches if necessary, add the swordfish steaks, making sure they've got a little space between one another. Cook until the steaks are a deep golden brown on one side, 5 to 7 minutes. Using a fish spatula or regular spatula, flip the steaks and cook until they are equally golden brown on the other side, another 4 to 6 minutes.

3 Transfer the fish to a large serving platter or even a baking dish. Add the garlic to the skillet and cook until just softened, a minute or two. Add the olive mixture and remove from heat.

4 Spoon some of the olive mixture over and let sit a few minutes to allow the sauce to marinate and really get to know that fish.

5 Scatter with the parsley and the remaining oregano, and serve with any extra olive mixture and the lemon halves for squeezing over.

Grilled Trout with Green Goddess Butter (A Whole Fish! Yes, You Can!)

serves 4 to 8

2–4 whole trout, branzino, or small
   black bass (12–14 ounces each),
   gutted and scaled
Kosher salt and freshly ground black
   pepper
A few sprigs of fresh savory, thyme,
   oregano, marjoram, or rosemary
1–2 tablespoons canola oil
Green Goddess Butter (page 124)
2 lemons or limes, halved
Flaky sea salt

NOTE *A whole fish is not as fussy as you think. A rather intuitive situation, perfectly cooked fish will fillet easily; the meat will effortlessly release from the bones simply by running a spoon or fork alongside the top of the spine. From there, you may have a few pin bones to deal with, which is not the end of the world, but definitely worth a mention. As for the rest of it: I don't eat the eyes, but I do eat the cheeks and think you should, too.*

Grilling a whole fish might sound like something you can't do, but let me say if you can grill a hot dog, you can grill a whole fish, especially something thin and manageably sized, like trout or branzino. Rather than seduce you with fancy flavor profiles and exotic ingredients, I want you to focus on the task at hand, which is just grilling the whole fish (which, for some, is already fancy and exotic enough). Apart from a good pair of tongs, all you'll need is confidence and a very hot grill. Considerably easier than grilling fillets, whole fish also screams festive and ambitious—what could be more fitting?

Once you master the process of preparing a whole fish simply, you can get as crazy as you want with sauces and marinades, and whatever else makes you happy. But here, all you really need to make it truly sing is to slather it with some sort of delicious butter, like this tangy, herby, salty Green Goddess Butter, and a healthy squeeze of citrus.

1 Heat a grill to medium-high.

2 Season the fish inside and out with salt and pepper. Stuff the inside with the herbs of your choosing and rub the outside of the fish with the oil. Place the fish directly on the grates with the spine facing you (this will make it easier to flip later). Let it grill, without moving or fussing, until the skin is charred, crisped, and fully cooked on one side, 6 to 8 minutes.

3 Test to see if the fish is ready to turn by using a spatula to flip the fish away from you onto its other side. A perfectly cooked fish will easily release from the grill; if it struggles, chances are it's not ready, so give it another minute. Once ready, flip the fish and continue cooking until the skin is crisped and the fish is fully cooked, another 6 to 8 minutes.

4 Use the spatula to transfer the fish onto one large serving platter (or two large plates). Spoon on some of the butter, letting it melt over the fish. Squeeze the citrus over and sprinkle with the flaky salt. Serve any extra butter alongside.

Buttered Salmon with Red Onion and Dill

serves 4 to 6

1 lemon

2 pounds skin-on or skinless salmon fillet

Kosher salt and freshly ground black pepper

6 tablespoons (¾ stick) unsalted butter

¼ cup olive oil, plus more for drizzling

½ small red onion, very thinly sliced into rings, divided

2 tablespoons brined capers, drained

1 cup fresh dill

2 tablespoons toasted sesame seeds (optional)

I would eat bagels with lox and cream cheese for every meal if I could, but since I can't (and honestly, really shouldn't), I have this salmon, which hits a lot of the same notes. There's plenty of red onion, briny capers, and lots of fresh dill. The sesame seeds at the end are optional, but I think they add even more toasty dimension to the brown butter sauce. Since there is a lot going on here flavor-wise, I recommend letting this dish be the loudest thing on the table and simply serving it with a perfect, herby salad (page 86), steamed broccoli (page 139), and maybe some excellent garlic bread (page 73).

1 Preheat the oven to 325°F. Thinly slice half the lemon and remove any seeds; save the other half for juicing.

2 Place the salmon on a rimmed baking sheet or in a large baking dish and season with salt and pepper.

3 Heat the butter in a medium skillet over medium-high heat. Cook, swirling occasionally until the butter has started to brown, 2 to 3 minutes. Add the olive oil, sliced lemon, and half the onion. Season with salt and pepper and cook, tossing occasionally, until the lemons and onion have started to brown and frizzle (you're looking for kind of crisped, rather than softened and caramelized), 2 to 3 minutes. Add the capers.

4 Pour the browned butter–lemon mixture over the salmon. Place it in the oven and roast until just cooked through but still medium-rare on the inside (it will look more translucent, less opaque), 12 to 15 minutes. Remove from the oven.

5 Meanwhile, toss together the dill and sesame seeds, if using, in a medium bowl and give a squeeze from the halved lemon; season with salt and pepper. Scatter on top of the salmon along with the remaining sliced onion.

Sungold Pasta with Lemony Shellfish, Garlic, and Pistachios

serves 4 to 6

1/3 cup olive oil, plus more as needed

8 garlic cloves, thinly sliced

1 large fennel bulb, thinly sliced, fronds reserved (if available)

Kosher salt and freshly ground black pepper

1 tablespoon fennel seeds, crushed, plus more for serving

1 teaspoon crushed red pepper flakes, plus more for serving

1 pound Sungold or cherry tomatoes, halved if especially large

12 ounces dried linguini or fettuccini

1/2 cup dry white wine

1½ pounds small littleneck or manila clams, cockles, or mussels, scrubbed and soaked

1½ pounds medium shrimp or prawns (head-on is optional), unpeeled or peeled

1/2 cup toasted pistachios, very finely chopped or ground

Flaky sea salt

1 lemon, halved

NOTE *In most recipes, I try to be flexible with the pasta shape that can be used, but here I play favorites and prefer a thick-ish noodle like linguini, perfect for a very sweet* Lady and the Tramp *moment, should you be presented with the opportunity.*

I have always been attracted to the abundant, theatrical nature of paella, but haven't ever been inclined to ever, you know, make it myself. Maybe I'm afraid of failure, but to me it's just always seemed like a lot of work and fussiness— things I try to avoid especially if I'm cooking for others. I mean, sure, if you've got a giant firepit overlooking a cerulean body of water, I will absolutely track down a giant paella pan and attempt to make some paella, but I can't offer promises on how it'll turn out. Instead, I'd opt for something that is as visually pleasing, requires a quarter of the effort, and, of course, involves pasta.

This is that pasta, which gets lightly tossed in a quick-cooking sweet/tart Sungold tomato sauce made with lots of caramelized fennel and garlic, and topped with the same sort of oceanic bounty you'd expect in a paella but without the work. It's an extremely impressive-looking situation, and is designed to be lingered over. It does not have to be piping-hot, and nobody needs to rush to eat the whole thing for fear it will not be as good once it cools down. It will be as good, and it will be as close to a perfect room-temperature pasta as you can get—a thing I never thought I'd say, but I can vouch for it.

1 Put a large pot of salted water on to boil.

2 Heat the olive oil in the largest skillet or wide, heavy-bottomed pot you have over medium-high heat. Add the garlic and fennel slices and season with salt and pepper. Cook, stirring occasionally, until the garlic and fennel are lightly browned and completely tender, 8 to 10 minutes.

3 Add the fennel seeds and crushed red pepper flakes, stirring to toast a bit. Add the tomatoes and season with salt and pepper. Cook until the tomatoes nearly all burst and are broken down into a jammy, sauce-y sauce, 10 to 12 minutes (using a wooden spoon or spatula to kind of gently crush them as they cook is a good idea).

NOTE *The pistachios are from a move I saw in Sicily, where most of the restaurants I went to used finely chopped Sicilian pistachios instead of cheese on their seafood pastas. To be clear, I am not one of those people who doesn't believe in cheese on seafood pasta (I very much do), but I also think that as an alternative, fatty pistachios mixed with salt are a good proxy and in this exact instance maybe even better than cheese (yes, I said it!).*

EAT WITH
Spicy Marinated Anchovies with Potato Chips (page 30)
+
A Very Fine Spritz (page 33)
+
Crushed Peas with Burrata and Black Olives (page 104)

4 Meanwhile, the pasta water should be boiling at this point, so go ahead and drop the pasta into the pot, cooking it to a nice al dente (timing will vary depending on pasta, so best to follow instructions on the package). Drain the pasta, reserving about ½ cup pasta water.

5 Add the wine and continue to cook until the sauce is reduced by about half, 4 to 5 minutes. Add the clams and if you have a lid, place it on top (if not, they will still open, just might take a few minutes more). Steam a few minutes just until they start to open (2 to 5 minutes, depending on size). Add the shrimp, season with salt and pepper, and toss to coat, continuing to cook until all the clams have opened and the shrimp are opaque and cooked through, another 3 to 5 minutes.

6 Since the skillet or pot is likely getting a little crowded, I like to toss my pasta with all of the tomato-y seafood business in the largest bowl I have, adding a bit of pasta water as I toss to keep things saucy. Season with salt, pepper, and more crushed red pepper flakes, if you like.

7 Transfer the mixture to a large serving bowl (or serve it straight from the mixing bowl) and top with the pistachios, flaky salt, fennel fronds, and, if you like, more fennel seeds and crushed red pepper flakes. Offer the lemon halves alongside for squeezing over.

Pot of Pasta with Broccoli Rabe and Chorizo Bread Crumbs

serves 6 to 8

1 pound fresh chorizo or spicy hot Italian sausage (about 4 links), casings removed

6 tablespoons olive oil, divided, plus more as needed

1½ cups fresh coarse bread crumbs (see page 14) or panko

Kosher salt and freshly ground black pepper

1 pound dried tube-shaped pasta, such as rigatoni or ziti

6 garlic cloves, thinly sliced

¼ cup tomato paste (1 4-ounce can)

1 large bunch of broccoli rabe, stems trimmed, coarsely chopped

Hunk of pecorino, parmesan, or ricotta salata, for grating

EAT WITH
Steamed Broccoli (page 139)
+
Lamb Chops for the Table (page 229)

Speaking from experience, I find that serving a giant pot of simple yet boldly flavored pasta to all your friends is about as crowd-pleasing as it gets, unless the crowd is full of people who don't eat pasta, and then you should really make something else. The perfect thing to make when you have no idea what to make, this pasta involves little to no technique—just a few very flavorful ingredients cooked together to spicy, tangy meaty, saucy perfection.

1 Cook the sausage in a large pot over medium-high heat, breaking up the meat with the back of a spoon, until browned, 5 to 8 minutes. Using a slotted spoon, remove the sausage, leaving the fat behind.

2 Add 3 tablespoons oil and the bread crumbs to the pot; season with salt and pepper. Cook, stirring frequently, until the bread crumbs are golden brown, 2 to 3 minutes. Transfer to a bowl.

3 Cook the pasta in a large pot of salted boiling water until just al dente. Drain, reserving at least 1 cup of the pasta water.

4 Meanwhile, heat the remaining 3 tablespoons olive oil in the pot, then add the garlic and cook, stirring occasionally, until it's toasted and golden brown, 2 to 3 minutes. Add the tomato paste and cook, stirring constantly, until it's a nice brick-red color and starts to stick a bit to the bottom of the pot, 2 to 3 minutes more.

5 Reduce the heat to medium-low and add the broccoli rabe, then season with salt and pepper. Cook, stirring occasionally, until it's all wilted and bright green, 3 to 5 minutes.

6 Add the pasta and chorizo back to the pot along with ½ cup of pasta water. Cook, stirring constantly, until each piece of pasta is coated nicely in the tomato-y, chorizo-y sauce.

7 Serve straight from the pot (or not), with toasted bread crumbs and pecorino for sprinkling over.

A Very Good Lasagna

serves 6 to 10

FOR THE SAUCE

2 tablespoons olive oil

1 large yellow onion, finely chopped

4 garlic cloves, finely chopped

6 anchovy fillets (optional)

Kosher salt and freshly ground black pepper

2 tablespoons tomato paste

1 (28-ounce) can whole peeled tomatoes

1 (28-ounce) can crushed tomatoes

FOR THE ASSEMBLY

1½ pounds fresh mozzarella, grated or shredded

16 ounces (2 cups) whole-milk ricotta

1 cup coarsely grated parmesan, plus more as desired

¼ cup heavy cream

Kosher salt and freshly ground black pepper

1 pound dried lasagna noodles (not the no-boil variety because I don't trust them)

Olive oil, for drizzling

In my quest to improve upon a classic lasagna, I fussed with it here and there, adding this, replacing that. But to be totally honest, at the end of a few failed attempts to improve upon the original, I realized the only thing I thought would improve it would be to construct a lasagna pan that was just all edges. But product invention isn't really my game.

For me, a very good lasagna isn't overly cheesy or too saucy or insanely indulgent—there should be a civilized ratio of pasta:sauce:cheese so that each slice feels satisfying but also balanced. While I do love a creamy lasagna, I find bechamels a bit unnecessary and instead use heavy cream in conjuction with the ricotta and mozzarella to keep things nice and saucy. So, here it is, a recipe for a Very Good Lasagna. Nothing insane, no sneaky anchovies (just kidding— there are anchovies) or expensive, hard-to-find cheeses. Just some good ol' basic stuff layered in a baking dish and baked until melty, bubbly, and satisfying as well.

I do have two pieces of advice: First, don't skip the two-bake process—the initial bake (foil on!) is the shorter of the two, only meant to melt the cheese and warm the sauce through, and the second bake (foil off!) is where things get good, and by good I mean golden brown, crispy-edged, and impossibly delicious. During this step the sauce will also continue to cook the al dente noodles, which makes for deeply seasoned pasta and eliminates any excess water, preventing a soggy, runny lasagna. Second, when you think you've baked it as long as you can, maybe bake it a little longer—the browner the better here.

1 Make the sauce. Heat the olive oil in a large, heavy-bottomed pot over medium heat. Add the onion, garlic, and anchovies and season with salt and pepper. Cook, stirring occasionally, until the onion is totally softened and translucent (without letting it brown), 8 to 10 minutes. Add the tomato paste and continue to cook, stirring, until the tomato paste has turned a deeper brick-red color, about 2 minutes.

2 Using your hands, crush the whole tomatoes into smaller, bite-sized pieces and add them and the crushed tomatoes to the pot, stirring to scrape up any bits from the bottom. Fill one of the tomato cans halfway with water and add it to the pot. Season with salt and pepper. Bring to a simmer and cook, stirring occasionally, until the tomato sauce has thickened and flavors have come together, 35 to 45 minutes. You want it to be as thick as tomato sauce from a jar— any looser and the lasagna will be too wet to cut into nice pieces.

3 Preheat the oven to 425°F and set a large pot of salted water to boil.

4 Assemble the lasagna. Set aside 1 cup mozzarella. In a medium bowl, combine the remaining mozzarella, the ricotta, parmesan, and cream; season with salt and pepper.

5 Cook the lasagna noodles in the boiling water until just softened (before al dente), 4 to 5 minutes. Drain and separate any noodles that are trying to stick together, drizzling them with a bit of olive oil to prevent them from sticking further.

6 Spoon a bit of sauce on the bottom of a 3-quart baking dish and top with a layer of noodles, avoiding any heavy overlap (some overlap is fine and inevitable). Top with about 1¼ cups of sauce, and dollop one-fourth of the cheese mixture over. Top with another layer of noodles and repeat three more times, ending with the last of the noodles (depending on size of the noodle/shape of the baking dish, you may have a few extra noodles) and the last of the sauce. Top with the reserved 1 cup mozzarella and more parmesan, if you like.

7 Cover loosely with aluminum foil and place the baking dish on a foil-lined rimmed baking sheet (to prevent any overflow from burning on the bottom of your oven). Bake until the pasta is completely tender and cooked through and the sauce is bubbling up around the edges, 25 to 30 minutes. Remove the foil and continue to bake until the lasagna is golden brown on top with frilly, crispy edges and corners, another 35 to 45 minutes. Let cool slightly before eating.

DO AHEAD The sauce can be made up to 1 week ahead, covered, and refrigerated. The lasagna can be baked up to 3 days ahead, wrapped tightly, and refrigerated (or up to 1 month, tightly wrapped and frozen). To reheat, cover with foil and bake at 375°F for 25 to 45 minutes.

Ricotta-Stuffed Shells with Burrata, Mushrooms, and Herbs

serves 6 to 10

2 pounds mixed fresh mushrooms,
  such as maitake, oyster,
  chanterelle, trumpet, or shiitake,
  torn or cut into bite-sized pieces

4 garlic cloves, well smashed

3 tablespoons olive oil, plus more as
  needed for the baking sheet and
  baking dish

Kosher salt and freshly ground black
  pepper

2 cups (16 ounces) full-fat ricotta

½ cup grated pecorino or parmesan,
  plus more as desired

1¼ cups heavy cream, divided

1 (12-ounce) box large dried shells

8 ounces burrata or mozzarella,
  torn into bite-sized pieces

1 cup fresh parsley, tender leaves
  and stems, coarsely chopped

½ cup finely chopped fresh chives

¼ cup fresh tarragon leaves

1 tablespoon grated lemon zest

EAT WITH
Vinegared Apples with Persimmon and
White Cheddar (page 103)
+
Garlicky Broccoli and Greens with
Hazelnut and Coriander (page 160)

My grandma loves to use the phrase "That's funny" for things that are decidedly not funny ha-ha but more like charming or cheeky. For example, her famous crudités feature crookneck squash with black peppercorns inserted as eyes to make them look like ducks and geese because she thinks "that's funny." Sure. Every time she buys a straw hat, she spray-paints it a very bright metallic silver because, according to her, "that's funny." You get the idea. Anyway, I definitely decided to include stuffed shells in this book because I think "that's funny," so I guess every day I am one day closer to becoming my grandma.

I am not going to lie and say that this is the kind of dish that can be slapped together moments before people show up to your house. But I will say that it's a *great* do-ahead (it can be assembled and refrigerated a day ahead), and once baked, it's the kind of quiet, unassuming main course that will always elicit "ooohs" and "aahhhs" and "OMG, I haven't had stuffed shells in *forever*." You could, of course, use another tube-ish shape, like cannelloni or something, or even layer this like a lasagna and use rigatoni or ziti.

1 Preheat the oven to 425°F.

2 Toss the mushrooms and garlic on a rimmed baking sheet with the olive oil and season with salt and pepper. Roast, tossing occasionally, until they're starting to brown and crisp, 15 to 20 minutes.

3 Meanwhile, combine the ricotta, pecorino, and ¾ cup cream in a medium bowl. Season with salt and pepper.

4 Cook the shells in a large pot of salted boiling water until just al dente. Drain and transfer to an oiled rimmed baking sheet. Toss the shells in a bit more oil, just to make sure they don't stick to one another as you're filling them.

NOTE *Asking your friends
to fill the shellls will save
you a lot of time, plus it
will give them something
to do other than eat all
your snacks.*

5 Using a spoon, fill each shell with the ricotta mixture—they should look pretty full, but don't be crazy, okay? You have a lot of shells to fill!

6 Drizzle a bit of olive oil in the bottom of a 2-quart baking dish or large cast-iron skillet (a 9 by 13-inch baking dish will work in a pinch, although it won't be as dramatic as a presentation). Place the shells in the baking dish, letting them overlap slightly, so each is as snug as a bug in a rug. Or a shell in a dish. Ha. Anyway. Scatter the burrata into the little in-between spots and top with the mushrooms. Pour the remaining ½ cup cream over everything.

7 Cover with foil and bake until the cheese is melted and everything is warmed through, 8 to 10 minutes. Remove the foil and continue to bake until the shells are sizzling around the edges and the mushrooms have miraculously gotten even darker and more caramelized looking, 15 to 20 minutes.

8 Meanwhile, combine the parsley, chives, tarragon, and lemon zest in a small bowl. Season with salt and pepper and drizzle with a little olive oil.

9 Top the pasta with the herb mixture, grating or shaving more pecorino over, and serve.

DO AHEAD The cheese mixture can be made a day ahead. The dish can be assembled a day ahead, wrapped tightly, and refrigerated. I wouldn't recommend baking this too far in advance, though, and reheating it, as the cheese has a tendency to dry out.

my favorite night is pizza night

Anyone who knows me knows how important pizza is to my soul, my personality, my body, my heart, my brain. Pizza is me, I am pizza. So, living in a place like New York, why would I go through the trouble of making my own when I have such good options literally everywhere? Well, that's a great question and I'm glad you asked. First, this book isn't for me, it's for you. And I'm guessing that at least a few of you don't live in New York but maybe want to have delicious pizza in your own home, without having to slide a frozen disc off a cardboard slab.

Second, even as someone who lives in a place with abundantly excellent options for 'za (nobody calls it that), I can say it is extremely fun to make your own. As I'm sure you can imagine, I am very picky when it comes to pizza and I have a *lot* of opinions (sauce ratio, texture and doneness of crust, toppings), so the idea that I just get to decide my own pizza destiny is—thrilling. Yes, I am a control freak, and by making my own pizza, I let that freak flag fly.

That all said, I am not a *pizzaiolo* (surprising, I know!). I have not studied pizza making in Rome and I've never been to Naples. Not only is my oven not fueled by wood but also it barely fits a half-sheet pan. But am I going to let any of that get in the way of my making my friends what I would consider to be a very good pizza in the privacy of my own home? No. The recipe that follows for this particular kind of pizza, which I would classify as a grandma style of sorts, starts with a fluffy, oily, spongey dough (the same dough that gets you the focaccia on page 70) that turns into a crispy-edged crust and takes kindly to an array of toppings. I myself am an extreme traditionalist and think that a cheese or pepperoni pizza is the pinnacle of perfection, but if you have an avant garde pizza preference, then you do you.

Throwing a pizza party in your home will earn you a lot of new friends. Here are some tips to avoid feeling overwhelmed.

Make the dough and sauce ahead. Make the dough the day before, if you can. Store it in the fridge, and when it's go time, transfer it to the sheet trays, let it proof another 30 to 40 minutes, add the toppings, and bake. The sauce can be prepared in 20 minutes or up to 1 month ahead and frozen; take your pick.

DIT (Do It Themselves). Grate (or slice) the mozzarella, tear the kale, slice the onions, pick the herbs, cut the meat, and set them all out along with the open tin of anchovies, jar of chiles, and other things you may want on the pizza. This encourages friends to live out their own pizza-topping fantasies.

Embrace the semi-homemade. Since you're putting all your love into the dough and sauce, everything else can be (and should be) store-bought.

264

Pizza Night

serves 8 to 12/makes 2 pizzas

4 garlic cloves, smashed

3 tablespoons olive oil, plus more
    for drizzling

1 28-ounce can whole peeled plum
    tomatoes, crushed by hand

Kosher salt and freshly ground pepper

Crushed red pepper flakes

Dough for Overnight Focaccia (page
    70), made up through step 3

FOR PEPPERONI PIE

Basic tomato sauce (see above)

8 oz. mozzarella cheese, grated or
    thinly sliced

2–4 oz. pepperoni, sopressata,
    coppa, or other spicy, cured meat

½ small red or yellow onion, thinly
    sliced (optional)

Olive oil, for drizzling

Flaky sea salt

FOR LEMONY GREENS PIE

1 cup whole-milk ricotta cheese

Kosher salt and freshly ground pepper

1 bunch kale, stems removed, leaves
    torn into 2-inch pieces

Olive oil, for drizzling

½ small red or yellow onion, thinly
    sliced (optional)

Finely grated parmesan or pecorino
    cheese

Flaky sea salt

1 cup mixed tender, leafy fresh
    herbs such as parsley, basil, mint,
    and chives

1 lemon, for zesting and juicing

Here you'll find a very basic pizza sauce—which is both simpler and quicker than a sauce for, say, lasagna (page 256)—plus a few options for how to top your pizza. These are just recommendations and, similarly to a Baked Potato Bar (page 147), Pizza Night is all about the toppings, so I hope you feel empowered and excited to stray, adapt, and tweak to suit your preferences. Regardless of combos, to achieve ultimate pizza success, always use less sauce, cheese, and toppings than you think (more is not more here; in fact, more will result in a heavy, doughy, soggy-bottomed pie) and bake it longer than you think (crispy crust, both edges and center, is what we are after).

1 Combine the garlic, olive oil, and tomatoes in a medium pot over medium heat. Season with salt, pepper, and crushed red pepper flakes. Bring to a simmer and cook until slightly less saucy than it was when you started, 15 to 20 minutes. Season again with salt, pepper, and red pepper flakes.

2 Divide the risen focaccia dough in half so that you've got two pieces. Pour enough olive oil into two rimmed baking sheets to generously coat the entire sheet and, using your hands, spread it all around. Turn each piece of dough onto a baking sheet and, using your hands, coax the dough into a flat, even layer. (It doesn't need to stretch to the exact size of the sheet pan; it'll puff up and fill in as it proofs and bakes.)

3 Drizzle the top with lots more olive oil and lightly drape a piece of plastic over the dough for its final nap, letting it rest in the warmest part of the room for another 30 to 45 minutes.

4 Preheat the oven to 450°F.

5 When you're ready to bake, the dough will look light, puffy, and buoyant. To test this, use your fingertips to press the dough lightly. It should bounce back ever so slightly (if it sinks and deflates, you've overproofed the dough and it might never

**Finely grated parmesan or pecorino
cheese**
**Impossibly tender roasted garlic
cloves sitting in a sea of olive oil**
**Spicy, oily Calabrian peppers, whole
or coarsely chopped**
Dried or fresh oregano
Nutritional yeast
Anchovy fillets

recover. But let's not assume the worst— and even at its worst, you'll still have something edible and you can call it flatbread). Using the tips of your fingers, lightly dimple the surface, kind of like you're playing the piano.

6 Top the dough as desired, using the suggested toppings.

DO AHEAD: Tomato sauce can be made up to 5 days ahead and refrigerated, or up to 2 months ahead and frozen (but it'll take longer to defrost than it will to make in the first place).

FOR PEPPERONI PIE

1 Spoon the tomato sauce onto the dough just enough to lightly coat, being mindful not to be heavy handed (or you'll get a soggy pie). Scatter with the mozzarella, pepperoni slices, and some onion, if you like. Drizzle with more olive oil, especially around the crust, and sprinkle with flaky salt.

2 Bake, rotating once halfway through, until the crust is totally golden, bubbly, and puffed; the cheese is melted and browning; and the pepperoni have filled with their own fiery orange fat, the best part of a pepperoni pizza, 30 to 35 minutes.

3 Once the pizza is out of the oven, dust it with parmesan or nutritional yeast, chopped Calabrian peppers or red pepper flakes and maybe some chopped fresh herbs, if you're wild about herbs (as I am). Let cool slightly before cutting and serving.

FOR LEMONY GREENS PIE

1 Season the ricotta with salt and pepper. Massage the kale with a drizzle of olive oil and season with salt and pepper.

2 Dollop the ricotta onto the dough and scatter with the kale and some onion, if you like. Grate some parmesan or pecorino over and season with salt and pepper. Drizzle with more olive oil, especially around the crust, and sprinkle with flaky salt.

3 Bake, rotating once halfway through, until the crust is totally golden, bubbly, and puffed, the kale is wilted and charred, and the onions are softened, 30 to 35 minutes.

4 Once the pizza is out of the oven, top it with fresh herbs, lemon zest, and maybe a few anchovies. Squeeze the lemon over and let cool slightly before cutting and serving.

**after
dinner**

I know what some of you are thinking.

Do I *have* to serve dessert? And the answer is no, you absolutely do not. I mean, you probably vacuumed before inviting all these people over, which is already a lot. Yet I am an enthusiastic sucker for ritual, and there is no greater ritual than the sweet snack at the end of a meal, a lovely punctuation mark to signal the close of an evening—the proverbial (sometimes literal) cherry on top.

Similar to those in the snack chapter, the recipes here are designed with do-ability in mind, given all the other things you've got going on. They're a combination of "you can bake this—yes, even you" recipes, kind-of-thrown-together recipes, and also simple ideas that aren't really recipes at all. Regardless, I'd describe all the desserts here as crowd-pleasing—familiar riffs on classics that I updated for my taste, which skews salty, tart, and bitter. For the procrastinators (raises hand), most of these recipes can be made day of and served that evening. For those who want to get ahead, you can do that, too, with most of these recipes.

If actual honest-to-god desserts just aren't your thing, there's also a very strong argument for serving a classy amaro as dessert, because, well, it's your party and you'll drink if you want to. Truly something for everyone.

Crushed Blackberry and Cornmeal Cake

serves 8 to 10

½ cup (1 stick) unsalted butter, melted, plus softened butter for greasing the pan and for serving (optional)

2 pints fresh blackberries, raspberries, or blueberries

⅓ cup plus 2 tablespoons granulated sugar

1 cup all-purpose flour

¾ cup medium-grind yellow cornmeal

2 teaspoons baking powder

¼ cup light brown sugar

1 teaspoon kosher salt

2 large eggs

½ cup buttermilk (see page 14)

¼ cup canola oil

Good-quality honey (optional)

I would call this a "snacking cake" rather than a true dessert cake, which to me implies that it's a lightly sweetened situation, made for nibbling and coffee drinking, and maybe a long lingering conversation about gratitude or the merits of leaving it all behind to go live in a cabin in the woods. If you like cornbread but wish it were sweeter and less crumbly, maybe studded with lots of sweet-tart crushed berries, then you will absolutely love this cake. And hey, if not, you'll probably still love this cake.

1 Preheat the oven to 350°F. Lightly grease a 9-inch round cake pan with softened butter or nonstick cooking spray.

2 Place the blackberries and 2 tablespoons granulated sugar in a medium bowl and, using your hands (or a fork), crush the berries just to break them up a bit and release their juices.

3 Whisk the flour, cornmeal, baking powder, brown sugar, salt, and remaining ⅓ cup granulated sugar in a medium bowl.

4 Whisk the eggs and buttermilk together in another medium bowl or measuring cup. Whisk into the dry ingredients until just barely combined, then add the melted butter and the oil, whisking until no obvious lumps or dry spots remain. Add half of the crushed berries and gently fold, encouraging the streaking of juices.

5 Pour the batter into the prepared cake pan and scatter the top with the remaining berries and their juices. Bake until the edges of the cake start to pull away from the sides of the pan and are turning a nice deep golden brown, 45 to 50 minutes. Let cool slightly before eating with some nice honey and softened butter, if you like.

DO AHEAD This cake is best eaten in the first 48 hours. Keep it wrapped tightly at room temperature.

Coconut Banana Cream Pudding

serves 8 to 12

FOR THE PUDDING

8 large egg yolks

⅓ cup cornstarch

¾ cup granulated sugar, divided

2 cups heavy cream

2 (14-ounce) cans full-fat coconut milk

Pinch of kosher salt

Pinch of ground turmeric (optional)

1 teaspoon vanilla extract (optional)

¼ cup light brown sugar

4 tablespoons (½ stick) unsalted butter, cut into 1-inch pieces, softened

FOR THE ASSEMBLY

2 cups heavy cream

½ cup confectioners' sugar

Pinch of kosher salt

1 cup full-fat Greek yogurt

6 firm bananas, peeled and thinly sliced

2 tablespoons fresh lime juice

1 (11-ounce) box Nilla wafers or graham crackers

Maraschino cherries (optional)

Toasted coconut flakes or chocolate for shaving (optional)

Pudding is like a very soft and comfortable sweater that you like wearing around the house but wouldn't necessarily wear to, say, a party. In other words, it's not much to look at, but layer that pudding with limey bananas and whipped tangy yogurt, and top it with a festive maraschino cherry, and all of a sudden it's like in the movies when the "nerdy girl" takes off her glasses, lets her hair down, and reveals that she was, indeed, "a total babe" this whole time.

The most annoying part of making this dessert is the fact that you've got to use a lot of bowls, which I admit is pretty annoying. So first and foremost, thanks for playing along; you may be spending the whole day washing bowls, but you won't be sorry at the end of it all, because you'll have a lot of delicious coconut banana cream pudding. Anyway, the great part about this whole thing is that from there, it's an extremely casual assembly. No need to measure or ration, no tools required other than a spoon, plus you can truly use anything you like to house the pudding—a fun bowl, a trifle dish, a springform pan, a bucket. Whatever you have will work, and it'll be great! Remember, this is fun, okay?

1 Make the pudding. Whisk the egg yolks, cornstarch, and half of the granulated sugar in a medium bowl until pale and fluffy.

2 Heat the cream, coconut milk, remaining granulated sugar, salt, and the turmeric and vanilla, if using, in a medium pot over medium heat. Stir and heat until just simmering.

3 Slowly and gradually whisk about half of the cream mixture into the egg yolk mixture (this is to prevent the egg yolks from cooking). Then, stir the warmed egg yolk mixture into the pot with the cream and, whisking constantly, cook until it thickens and starts to bubble up and look like something that is so hot it could hurt you if it touched your skin (it can, so be careful!!!), 3 to 5 minutes.

(recipe continues)

4 Remove from the heat and whisk in the brown sugar and butter, whisking, whisking, whisking until the brown sugar has dissolved and the butter has melted.

5 Transfer the pudding to a baking dish (you can use a bowl if you don't have one, but basically this pudding should cool as quickly as possible so you want to use something wider than it is deep). Place plastic wrap directly on top of the pudding (to prevent that inevitable weird pudding skin) and place in the refrigerator to cool completely, at least 1 hour (depending on your fridge).

6 Assemble the dessert. Using an electric mixer or a whisk and good ol' fashioned elbow grease, whip the cream, confectioners' sugar, and salt in a medium bowl until medium-stiff peaks form. Gently whisk in the yogurt.

7 Toss the bananas and lime juice together in a medium bowl. This will make them taste very good and prevent browning.

8 Take out whatever fun vessel you'll be using for this assembly and spoon a bit of the coconut pudding on the bottom, followed by a layer of wafers, followed by a layer of bananas, followed by a layer of whipped cream mixture. Repeat this until you've filled the whole vessel, ending with the whipped cream. Do not worry about getting the layers totally even, that is not the point; just eyeball it to make sure you won't run out of anything while building the layers (but if you did, not the end of the world).

9 Chill the assembled pudding at least 2 hours, until everything is set and kind of settled into each other. When you're ready to serve, top with whatever you feel like—say, a maraschino cherry, toasted coconut flakes, or even some shaved chocolate. Serve with a large serving spoon and a few bowls, or just set out multiple spoons and eat directly out of the vessel. We're all friends here!

DO AHEAD The filling can be made up to 3 days ahead, wrapped, and refrigerated. The banana pudding can be assembled a day ahead—any more than that and the wafers will become almost "too soft," if there is such a thing.

Sour Cherry and Sesame Galette

serves 6 to 8

All-purpose flour, for dusting
1 recipe (2 discs) The Only Pie Crust
**   (page 311)**
3 pounds fresh sour cherries, pitted
¾ cup plus 3 tablespoons sugar
1 tablespoon fresh lemon or lime
**   zest, plus 2 tablespoons fresh**
**   lime or lemon juice**
⅓ cup tahini
1 large egg, lightly beaten with
**   1 teaspoon water**
3 tablespoons white sesame seeds
Flaky sea salt

NOTE *An excellent task to outsource, pitting cherries is quite literally the pits. Note that most fruit will work here, just cut into cherry-sized pieces before proceeding.*

I typically do not condone the double-crust galette (because, then, isn't it just a pie?), but the idea for this recipe came about after attempting to eat a galette with juicy cherries and having the cherries fall all over me, staining my clothes. *"What if instead of a galette, it was a giant pop tart?"* I thought. So I present to you something that is galette in spirit, pop tart in theory, and pepperoni pizza in appearance (which was an accident, but now that I've said it, you can't un-see it).

Because it is still galette in spirit, it should have enough holes cut from the top so that the filling can bubble up and breathe, and the whole thing can maintain what makes a galette great, which is the correct ratio of filling to crust. If you don't own tiny cookie cutters for cutting out small holes, things like a water bottle cap work surprisingly well. Alternatively, use a knife to make dramatically thick slits.

1 Preheat the oven to 400°F.

2 Lightly flour a large work surface. Working with 1 disc of dough at a time, roll out 2 circles about 16 inches each in diameter, give or take an inch or two. Place one crust on a parchment-lined rimmed baking sheet and have the other alongside on the work surface.

3 Working with the crust on the work surface, use a tiny circle/square/rectangle/triangle/heart/star cutter (about 1 inch) or the cap of a plastic water bottle, or whatever sharp-edged circle is close to 1 inch in diameter, to cut out many small shapes, taking care to leave about a 3-inch border of uncut dough. You can save these scraps and make snacks later or eat the raw dough, which is something I do (and which I can't technically advise doing, but just letting you know it is delicious).

(recipe continues)

4 Toss the cherries, ¾ cup of the sugar, and the lemon zest and juice in a large bowl.

5 Spread the tahini on the crust that's on the baking sheet, leaving a 3-inch border all around (like you're saucing a pizza!). Place the cherries on top of the tahini, making sure they stay within that 3-inch border.

6 Brush the edges of the crust with the egg wash, then place the other crust with the holes on top of the fruit, pressing to make sure the plain edges stick together. Fold the edges up all around onto each other, pressing with each fold to create a seal (like if you were making a regular galette). Brush the entire top with the egg wash, then sprinkle with the sesame seeds, the remaining 3 tablespoons sugar, and a bit of flaky salt.

7 Bake the galette, rotating if your oven has hot spots, until the top crust is beginning to turn a nice golden brown and the filling starts to bubble up slightly, 20 to 25 minutes. Reduce the temperature of the oven to 375°F and continue to bake until the crust is baked through and is the color of a deeply golden brown, well-baked croissant, another 20 to 25 minutes.

8 Let the galette cool slightly before slicing into wedges, which will look like pepperoni pizza slices. Do not apologize for this!

DO AHEAD Galette can be baked up to 2 days ahead, wrapped tightly, and stored at room temperature.

Upside-Down Apricot Tart

serves 6 to 8

¼ cup honey

¼ cup sugar

2 tablespoons water

2 tablespoons unsalted butter

1 tablespoon apple cider vinegar

Flaky sea salt

1 pound fresh apricots or plums
(about 6 apricots or 4 plums),
halved lengthwise and pitted

1 (14-ounce) box puff pastry
(1 sheet)

All-purpose flour, for dusting

¼ cup pistachios, very finely
chopped (optional)

Ice cream or whipped cream
(optional)

Puff pastry is one of those store-bought ingredients that makes you look like a better baker than you are. There are varying degrees of quality among the brands to be found in grocery stores (I prefer Dufour), but honestly most do their job of puffing up to a tall, crispy pastry. While I do love the *idea* of making my own, I'm uh . . . never gonna do that. But what I will do is open a package, remove the dough, flatten it out on a counter, place it atop some caramelized fruit, and bake it until it gets all puffed, golden, and shatteringly crispy. Sure, you could use apples, but they never really achieve what an apricot can do, which is give you something that is perfectly jammy, joyfully acidic, and fantastically saucy, all at once. Plus, no pre-bake required.

For those paying attention, yes, you could call this a *tarte tatin*, but I'm calling it an upside-down apricot tart because to me, *tarte tatin* is a specific thing made with apples. Since this isn't that, I rebranded out of respect. Anyway, this is the perfect dessert for those who can bake and those who can't, since regardless of what goes on top, the combination of apricots + butter + sugar + flaky pastry in any preparation is not bad—in fact, it is very good. (Note: It *can* also be made with plums! That's cool, right?)

1 Preheat the oven to 425°F.

2 Heat the honey, sugar, and water in a small pot over medium-high heat. Cook, stirring occasionally, until the mixture goes from a pale golden brown watery syrup to a dark amber caramel (you're making a caramel, but because of the honey, it can be hard to tell when the color changes, so think the color of good-quality maple syrup).

3 Remove from heat and, using a wooden spoon or spatula, add the butter, vinegar, and a pinch of flaky salt, letting it bubble up, stirring and swirling to incorporate. Pour this now-opaque caramel into a 9- or 10-inch round cake pan, tart pan, or skillet (the possibilities are endless!), swirling to make sure it evenly coats the bottom of the pan.

4 Lay the apricots cut side down in the pan, letting them overlap slightly, if needed. If you seem to have too many apricots to fit in the pan you have, enjoy the rest as a snack.

5 Take the puff pastry out of the box and place it on a lightly floured work surface. Depending on the brand, it'll likely be a rectangle or a square, so lightly roll the edges to a circle-ish shape and smooth any obvious creases so that the pastry bakes evenly. Using scissors or a knife, trim the pastry so that it's about 1 inch larger than the circumference of the pan (it does not have to be a perfect circle). Place the pastry on top of the apricots, letting it slump up the sides but not hang over (the pastry will shrink as it bakes, so you need a bit of excess dough to compensate).

6 Bake until the pastry is puffed and starting to turn a light golden brown (think the color of shortbread), 15 to 20 minutes. Reduce the temperature to 375°F and continue to bake until the pastry looks more like a well-baked croissant and the fruit below is bubbling furiously and deliciously, another 25 to 30 minutes.

7 Remove from the oven and let rest for 10 to 15 minutes, just to cool the caramel a bit. To invert, place a plate that is at least as large as the pan you're using (but better if it's a little larger) on top of the pastry. With dish towels or oven mitts, flip the tart over so that the bottom is now the top. Pick up the pan, leaving the fruit and delicious crust and tangy sauce to drip all over everything.

8 Serve with pistachios and more flaky salt sprinkled over, or with ice cream or whipped cream on the side, or with literally nothing at all, because it is truly perfect as is.

DO AHEAD You can bake this tart a few hours ahead, but do not invert it until you're ready to serve. If the caramel has set too firmly to release from the pan, pop it in a 375°F oven for 5 minutes or so to warm and loosen up.

Casual Apple Tart with Caramelized Buttermilk

serves 4 to 6

6 tablespoons (¾ stick) unsalted
   butter
½ teaspoon ground cinnamon,
   cardamom, and/or ginger
   (optional)
½ recipe (1 disc) The Only Pie Crust
   (page 311)
All-purpose flour, for dusting
2 pounds firm tart apples (such as
   Pink Lady, Honeycrisp, Winesap,
   or Gold Rush), unpeeled, cored,
   and sliced ¼ inch thick
¼ cup plus 2 tablespoons sugar
⅓ cup buttermilk (see page 14)
Flaky sea salt
Freshly ground black pepper

NOTE *The secret upgrade
here is the buttermilk, which is
used instead of an egg wash
(although that would work,
of course). As the tart bakes,
the sugars in the buttermilk
caramelize, lending a
crystallized texture and faintly
tart but deeply milky flavor—
perfect with lightly cinnamon-
flavored and delightfully tender
apples, which reminds me
every time of eating a bowl of
Cinnamon Toast Crunch. The
highest of compliments.*

There are a lot of things you can do with apples, but none of them interests me as much as scattering them onto a flaky crust and baking them till they're tender. I call this a casual tart rather than any number of other names that would be fitting, because I want you to feel free to slice the apples however you want, roll the dough into whatever shape pleases you, and carry on to make your own version of what is surely a casual (and delicious) apple tart.

1 Preheat the oven to 400°F.

2 Melt the butter in a small pot over medium heat, swirling occasionally, until melted and starting to foam up and brown, 3 to 4 minutes (whisk the butter from time to time so that the solids don't stick to the bottom). Remove from the heat, add the spices (if using), and set aside.

3 Gently roll out the dough (1 disc) onto a lightly floured piece of parchment paper to about ⅛-inch thickness in any shape you like (irregular circle, rectangle, square, whatever!).

4 Leaving a 2-inch border on all sides, arrange the apples on top, either preciously shingled or haphazardly scattered. Brush the apples with the browned butter and sprinkle with ¼ cup of the sugar.

5 Fold the edges of the dough up over the apples and brush the dough with the buttermilk followed by the remaining 2 tablespoons sugar. Sprinkle everything with flaky sea salt and black pepper. Transfer the tart on the parchment to a rimmed baking sheet and bake until the entire crust is deeply golden brown and the apples are tender and cooked through, 45 to 50 minutes. Let cool before slicing and eating in any manner that feels casual and appropriate.

DO AHEAD Tart can be baked 2 days ahead, wrapped tightly, and kept at room temperature.

fruit on ice

Unless you're Chez Panisse, the concept of serving simple fruit for dessert could be mistaken as a bit phoned in. Fruit *on ice*, however, like anything "on ice," seems a bit more magical, a bit more spectacular. Plus, "on ice" is half décor (so sparkly!), half practical (sooo cold!). Doing this is obviously simple, since as the title would suggest, all you need is fruit and ice.

The fruit should be ripe and juicy, served raw and unadulterated. If the fruit is already bite-sized, like perfect sour cherries or lovely, tiny plums, then they can be served whole. If the fruit is large, like pineapple or watermelon, then it should be cut into individual single-serve wedges or long, dramatic spears. If the fruit has a tendency to turn brown as it sits (apples, pears), they would like a squeeze of lemon or lime to keep them looking nice. Fruit that is too small, like blueberries, should be avoided, as you'll spend all your time digging around in very cold ice looking for a tiny berry, which would be about as fun as it sounds. Mushy fruit like bananas are not allowed here.

The ice itself should not be too small or it will melt too quickly (this is not a snow cone, this is Fruit on Ice), nor should it be too large, or the fruit won't properly nestle in, chilling as intended (save the large cubes for cocktails). Aside from that, all you need is a (preferably wide, shallow) bowl large enough to hold all your Fruit on Ice dreams. As the ice melts, it's nice to add more as needed and get rid of any excess water so the fruit doesn't end up sitting in a swimming pool of water.

Crispy Chocolate Cake with Hazelnut and Sour Cream

serves 8 to 10

FOR THE CAKE

½ cup (1 stick) unsalted butter, plus more for greasing the pan

¾ cup plus 2 tablespoons granulated sugar, plus more for the pan

8 ounces bittersweet chocolate, at least 67% cacao, finely chopped

½ cup Nutella, hazelnut spread, almond butter, or tahini (see Note)

6 large eggs

½ cup hazelnut or almond flour

2 tablespoons unsweetened cocoa powder

1 teaspoon kosher salt

FOR THE TOPPING/ACCOMPANIMENT

1 cup heavy cream

¼ cup confectioners' sugar

Pinch of kosher salt

1 cup sour cream

¼ cup Nutella

Brandied, maraschino, or Luxardo cherries (optional)

NOTE *Using an unsweetened spread like almond butter or tahini will give you a slightly less sweet version of this cake, which for my taste, is still perfectly sweet enough.*

I first published this recipe in *Bon Appétit* circa 2013 (a.k.a. four thousand years ago), but since then I've made it even better. It's got a crispy, crackly exterior with a magical, chocolatey interior that's somehow simultaneously dense and light as hell. It's also easy to make, with near-foolproof results.

Yes, the original version (inspired by Richard Sax's "Cloud Cake") was excellent, but this version is, dare I say, Much Better. First, there is Nutella in it; second, well, if you didn't hear me the first time, I have put Nutella in it; third, I have also put Nutella in the whipped sour cream topping. In another world, that might be gilding the lily, but not in this world! Less sexily, there is also the addition of nut flour, which gives the whole thing a bit more body with a denser-in-a-good-way texture.

Yes, this cake is gluten-free, but not by design, which is to say I would never call this a gluten-free cake, lest the gluten lovers feel like they are missing out on something potentially better (there isn't).

1 Preheat the oven to 350°F. Lightly grease a 9-inch springform pan with softened butter or nonstick cooking spray. (You can use any 9-inch cake pan, but line it with parchment paper with some overhang so you can easily remove the finished cake.) Sprinkle the inside with sugar and rotate the pan to coat the bottom and sides evenly; tap out excess.

2 Make the cake. Combine the chocolate, Nutella, and butter in a large heatproof bowl. Set the bowl over a small pot of simmering water and heat, stirring often, until the chocolate and butter have melted and you can stir everything together to a smooth, creamy mixture. Remove from the heat and set aside. (Alternatively, microwave in 30-second increments until evenly melted.)

3 Separate 4 of the eggs, placing the whites in a large mixing bowl (either a bowl fitted for a stand mixer or a bowl large enough to handle a hand mixer). Place the yolks in another large bowl and add the hazelnut flour, cocoa powder, salt, and the remaining 2 whole eggs and whisk to blend well. Using a spatula, gently and gradually mix the egg yolk mixture into the melted chocolate mixture (don't use a whisk here; the batter is quite thick and will get stuck in the wires).

4 With the mixer on high, beat the egg whites. When they start to get light and foamy, gradually add ¾ cup sugar, a tablespoon or two at a time, and continue to beat until egg whites have tripled in volume and are light, fluffy, opaque, and hold stiff peaks. They should look like a very good meringue that you could frost a cake with (that's not what you'll be doing, but just saying).

5 Using a spatula, gently fold the egg whites into the chocolate mixture until just combined and no obvious white streaks remain (this will look cool—maybe take a picture!); avoid overmixing (that would deflate all that air you worked so hard to build into those egg whites).

6 Pour the batter into the prepared pan and smooth the top. Sprinkle with the remaining 2 tablespoons granulated sugar and bake until the edges begin to pull away from the sides of the pan and the top looks puffed and lightly cracked, like a soufflé (it should still have a little jiggle), 35 to 40 minutes.

7 Let cool completely (if you have a wire rack, use it). During this time, something seemingly tragic will happen—the center of the cake will collapse, causing further cracking around the edges. This is the intended effect, so don't worry—it's where those crispy edges come from, the reason we are all here.

8 Prepare the topping/accompaniment. Using an electric mixer (or a good old-fashioned whisk and elbow grease), whip the cream, confectioners' sugar, and salt in a medium bowl until you've got medium-stiff peaks, then whisk in the sour cream. For a streaky effect, fold in the Nutella using a spatula or if, you know, who cares, just whisk it in. Use this mixture to top the cake, but I prefer to eat it on the side (so as to not ruin the cake's crispy texture) with some delicious cherries for snacking on in between bites.

DO AHEAD You can bake this cake up to 2 days ahead, wrap it tightly, and store at room temperature.

Sweet and Salty Cream Cheese Tart

serves 8 to 10

FOR THE CRUST

5 ounces Ritz crackers or Nilla wafers (see Note)

2 tablespoons light brown sugar

4 tablespoons (½ stick) unsalted butter, melted

Pinch of kosher salt

FOR THE FILLING

1 pound (2 8-ounce packages) full-fat cream cheese, preferably room temperature, or 2 cups labne

1 cup sour cream or full-fat Greek yogurt

½ cup granulated sugar

2 large eggs

3 tablespoons fresh grapefruit, lemon, lime, or orange juice

Flaky sea salt

Fresh citrus, halved or sliced (optional)

Ask me what my dream dessert is and I'll tell you it's cheese. Just cheese (my first love), or any dessert that heavily features the stuff, such as cheesecake. However, and stay with me here, I truly believe that a classic cheesecake is just: Too. Much. Cheesecake. My perfect specimen has a thicker crust (made with something buttery, salty, and sandy-crumbed like Ritz crackers or Nilla Wafers) and about half the filling as a traditional one, yielding a better crust-to-filling ratio. (You can eat a lot more slices that way.)

While cream cheese is the default here since it's the most widely available, I will say that if you are able to make this tart with labne, you will be very glad you did. The tart will be a bit saltier, a touch smoother, and a whole lot tangier. Oh, and you absolutely do not need to bake this tart in a water bath, a technique that gets filed directly under "Yeah, I'm not gonna do that."

1 Preheat the oven to 325°F.

2 Make the crust. Pulse the crackers in a food processor until you've got a fine crumb (crumb, not powder!); you can also do this by hand by placing the crackers in a resealable bag and crushing or smashing with a skillet or rolling pin. Transfer to a medium bowl and add the brown sugar and butter, followed by the salt. Using your hands, mix until the crumbs are evenly coated and you have a wet sand texture.

4 Press the crust into an unlined 9-inch tart or springform pan, or cake pan lined with parchment. You can use a lined 8-inch square baking pan here, although expect a slightly thicker outcome (maybe that is your preference). Using the bottom of a measuring cup or small bowl, really press the crumb mixture in there—otherwise it can be challenging to cut later on.

NOTE *I am generally a fair and flexible person when it comes to ingredients. However, with the advent of private label "vanilla wafers" and "Ritz-esque" crackers, I have to mention that I tested this recipe with only name brands (Nabisco, in both cases), which I find to be reliable. I cannot attest to the success with any other brand, unfortunately, so proceed at your own risk.*

5 Bake the crust until it's lightly golden brown at the edges (it gets baked one more time, so best not to overdo it here), 10 to 15 minutes.

6 Make the filling. Combine the cream cheese, sour cream, and granulated sugar in the bowl of a food processor and process until impossibly smooth and well blended, scraping down the sides as needed to incorporate any stubborn chunks of cream cheese. Add the eggs, grapefruit juice, and a pinch of salt, and keep processing until it's even smoother and creamier than before (a miracle!).

7 Pour into the baked crust and bake until the whole thing is set and no longer jiggles when tapped, 25 to 35 minutes (it should not brown at all).

8 Turn the oven off and open the door a crack. Let the tart sit in there for about 15 minutes before transferring it to a wire rack on a counter to cool completely. Then place in the fridge to chill at least 1 hour (this gradual cooling is to prevent any unsightly cracks from appearing on the surface, which can happen when there is a sudden or drastic change in temperature).

9 To serve, sprinkle with a little flaky salt and serve with some fresh citrus of your choosing, if you like.

DO AHEAD Tart can be baked up to 3 days ahead, wrapped tightly, and refrigerated. Cream cheese tends to pick up what I affectionately call "fridge flavors" easily, so make sure it's really wrapped well.

Sheet Cake with Mascarpone and Coffee

serves 6 to 10

FOR THE CREAM
4 large egg yolks
½ cup sugar, divided
½ cup heavy cream
Kosher salt
Vanilla bean, split and seeds scraped (optional)
2 cups (16 ounces) mascarpone

FOR THE ASSEMBLY
1¾ cups good espresso or very strong coffee (see Note)
2 tablespoons rum, whiskey, or cognac
2 tablespoons unsweetened cocoa powder, divided
Almost Angel Food Cake (page 310) or 1 (7-ounce) package of ladyfingers (about 24)

NOTE *I get this at a coffee shop since I never seem to brew my coffee strong enough.*

If this feels like a trick to get you to make tiramisu, then you are correct. Many people don't like tiramisu, and that's because often it is bad. Too dry or too soggy, too sweet or too boozy—there's a lot that can go wrong. But if you think of it as a very good angel food cake delicately soaked with bitter espresso and layered with a barely sweetened, custardy, pillowy mascarpone, then you may be open to the possibility that you do, indeed, love tiramisu.

I first saw this "instead of individual cakes, make one big cake" technique employed by one of my favorite people and chefs, Brooks Headley, of Superiority Burger fame. Not only does it make more sense to soak one large thing rather than dip many small things, it makes for a better cake-to-cream ratio and, thus, more enjoyable to eat.

1 Make the cream. Using a stand mixer or an electric hand beater, in a medium bowl, whip the egg yolks and ¼ cup sugar until very pale yellow, tripled in volume, and holds a slight ribbon when the beaters are lifted. Transfer to a large bowl.

2 Whip the cream, a pinch of salt, the vanilla bean, if using, and the remaining ¼ cup sugar in the mixer bowl until you've got soft peaks. Add the mascarpone and continue to whip until you've got a soft, pillowy mixture with medium peaks. Fold the egg yolk mixture into the cream mixture.

3 Assemble. Combine the espresso and rum in a small bowl. Using a sifter or powdered sugar shaker, dust the bottom of a 2-quart baking dish with 1 tablespoon of the cocoa powder.

4 Place half of the cake (or a layer of ladyfingers) in the bottom of the baking dish and, using a spoon or pastry brush, douse with half the espresso mixture. Evenly spread half the mascarpone mixture onto the cake, and repeat with the remaining cake, espresso, and mascarpone mixtures. Dust the top layer with the remaining tablespoon of cocoa powder. Chill for at least 4 hours before serving.

DO AHEAD You can make this 1 to 2 days ahead.

Salted Honey Panna Cotta with Crushed Raspberries

serves 6 to 10

1 (¼-ounce) envelope unflavored
    gelatin powder
¼ cup water
3 cups heavy cream, divided
½ cup plus 2 tablespoons honey,
    plus more for garnish
1 cup buttermilk (see page 14)
1 cup sour cream
½ vanilla bean, split and seeds
    scraped (optional)
Pinch of kosher salt
6 ounces fresh raspberries
1 tablespoon apple cider vinegar, or
    fresh lime or lemon juice

NOTE *Panna cotta translates directly to "cooked cream," but the funny thing is that the cream in a panna cotta should never be cooked, as that would change the flavor of the cream. Isn't that funny? I mean, not funny ha-ha, but, you know.*

Panna cotta is the ultimate low-fuss, high-reward dessert. It's a bit like a slice of pizza: even when it's mediocre, it's still pretty good, but when it's great, it's transcendent. To qualify as such, it's gotta be barely set and just sweet enough. It should go without saying that the quality of the dairy is important here, but as anyone who's opened a fresh carton of heavy cream and licked the top knows, any heavy cream, without even trying, is spectacular.

While these can be made in any small bowl or glass you own, aim for short and wide as opposed to tall and thin for the fastest chilling and best eating experience.

1 Sprinkle the envelope of gelatin over the water and let sit 2 or 3 minutes to soften and hydrate (so that it doesn't clump).

2 Add the squishy gelatin to a small pot along with ½ cup cream and ½ cup honey. Heat over low heat, swirling the pot until the gelatin is totally dissolved, making sure not to simmer.

3 Gently whisk the buttermilk, sour cream, vanilla, if using, remaining 2½ cups cream, and a pinch of salt in a large bowl.

4 Slowly whisk the warm gelatin mixture into the buttermilk mixture, taking care not to whisk too hard or else it'll trap air bubbles (you don't want that). Divide the mixture among 6 to 10 glasses. Chill until the panna cotta is set, at least 1 hour.

5 Meanwhile, place the raspberries, vinegar, and remaining 2 tablespoons honey in a medium bowl. Using a fork, crush the fruit to release the juices. Serve the panna cotta topped with the crushed raspberry mixture, additional honey, or nothing at all.

DO AHEAD The panna cotta mixture can be made 5 days ahead; it keeps well in a plastic container and can be warmed to a liquid, poured into individual serving glasses, and chilled before serving.

Torn Plum Browned-Butter Cake

serves 6 to 8

¾ cup (1½ sticks) unsalted butter
¾ cup almond flour
½ cup all-purpose flour
½ teaspoon kosher salt
1¼ cups confectioners' sugar, plus
more for the top
5 large egg whites
¼ cup honey
1½ pounds plums, pitted and torn
or cut into bite-sized pieces
(see Note)
¼ cup demerara sugar

NOTE *I have a fondness for plums because their color speaks to my soul, especially when baked and they get all jammy and tie-dyed looking. But you can feel good about using any excruciatingly ripe stone fruit, berries, or pears you can get your hands on.*

If you are a fan of summer desserts, you may be familiar with Marian Burros's famous Plum Torte, first published in the *New York Times* in 1983. Her dessert and this cake both feature plums sunken into a batter and baked, but they are very different. For anyone keeping track, the batter here, featuring egg whites, browned butter, and almond flour, is more financier (chewy, dense, buttery, nutty) than a torte (which has a more straightforward pound cake texture). Both are excellent and should coexist in your summer baking repertoire.

1 Preheat the oven to 375°F. Spray a 2-quart baking dish or an 8- or 9-inch cake pan with nonstick cooking spray. Line with parchment paper, if you like.

2 Melt the butter in a small pot over medium heat, swirling occasionally, until melted and starting to foam and brown, 3 to 4 minutes (whisking occasionally so the solids don't stick to the bottom of the pot). Let cool.

3 Whisk the flours, salt, and confectioners' sugar in a large bowl. Add the egg whites and honey, and whisk to blend until no lumps remain.

4 Using a spatula, gently fold in the browned butter.

5 Pour the batter into the prepared pan. Scatter the plums over, making sure they're evenly distributed (whether the torn sides are up or down doesn't matter), and sprinkle with the demerara sugar.

6 Bake, rotating the cake once, until the edges are deeply browned, 35 to 40 minutes. Remove from the oven and let cool slightly before cutting into whatever shapes your heart desires.

DO AHEAD Cake can be baked up to 3 days ahead, wrapped tightly, and stored at room temperature.

Hibiscus-Roasted Peaches with Brown-Sugar Bread Crumbs

serves 4 to 8

FOR THE BREAD CRUMBS

4 tablespoons unsalted butter

1½ cups coarse fresh bread crumbs (see page 14) or panko

¼ cup light brown sugar

Flaky sea salt

FOR THE PEACHES AND ASSEMBLY

2 pounds ripe peaches or nectarines, halved and pitted

½ cup granulated sugar, plus more as needed (see Note)

¼ cup hibiscus (Jamaica) flowers (see Note)

2 tablespoons fresh lemon juice

2 tablespoons water

Vanilla or whatever flavor ice cream you fancy

NOTE *If the peaches you're using are especially tart or hard and out of season, then you may want to add another tablespoon or two of sugar to compensate.*

Dried hibiscus flowers (a.k.a. sorrel) are available in Latin and Caribbean grocery stores and in the tea aisle at most other grocery stores.

For all this talk about how I don't care for sweets, I have an alarming amount of cereal that could be described as "probably for children" in my pantry. Since that's filed under "personal snack," I made these salty, lightly sweetened, buttery bread crumbs to serve to and eat in front of others. They are perfect eaten a million different ways (including out of hand), but I find them best eaten as I would cereal: swimming in a pool of dairy.

The peaches are also a very "nothing fancy" mood, taking no time to prepare but looking and tasting extremely special. Served warm, room temperature, or chilled, they are roasted just long enough to get their juices flowing, creating a highly tangy, vibrantly fuchsia sauce—ideal for spooning over ice cream and sprinkling with those bread crumbs I can't stop talking about.

1 Make the bread crumbs. Melt the butter in a large skillet over medium heat. Add the fresh bread crumbs and toss to coat. Cook, stirring occasionally, until the bread crumbs start to brown, 3 to 4 minutes. Add the brown sugar and continue to cook until the brown sugar has begun to caramelize as the bread crumbs take on a deep golden brown color, another 2 to 3 minutes. Remove from the heat and season with flaky salt.

2 Preheat the oven to 400°F.

3 For the peaches and assembly. Place the peaches, cut side down, in a large baking dish. Sprinkle with the sugar and add the hibiscus, lemon juice, and water.

4 Roast the peaches, without turning, until the edges are bubbling and a good, syrupy sauce has formed in the baking dish, 15 to 20 minutes. Remove from the oven and let cool. Serve the peaches over ice cream and topped with bread crumbs.

DO AHEAD Bread crumbs can be made up to 4 days ahead, wrapped, and stored at room temperature. Peaches can be roasted up to 2 days ahead, covered, and refrigerated.

after-dinner drinks

More often than not, instead of cake, I will be offering you a classy, boozy beverage for dessert. Specifically a syrupy, botanical-laced amaro or punchy, smooth-not-smoky mezcal. But like cake, there is still a ritualistic element to this end-of-the-night beverage (and I love a ritual), plus some herbal liqueurs can most definitely work to aid digestion (it's science!). That, and a woman cannot survive on natural wine alone. (I have tried, and it did not go well.) Having a few nice, unique bottles in your possession means that even if you didn't make anything for dessert, you'll always have a little sweet something to bring out at the end of a meal—plus the bottles, which last an eternity, will look great on your shelf.

Along with the bottles of amaro, mezcal, scotch, or whiskey, I'll set out a few tiny glasses, a bowl of ice and, depending on how things went up until that point, perhaps a little plate of sliced oranges or lemon peels.

As long as you're sipping (never slamming), there's no wrong or right way to drink these drinks (straight up, on the rocks, with a twist, without). Each person can customize their experience based on preference. For those not indulging or who perhaps need a little end-of-night break, I like to offer non-alcoholic digestive bitters dashed into club soda over ice.

Since all of these spirits' flavor profiles and bitterness levels can vary wildly, I recommend asking someone at a wine or spirits store you trust and tell them what kinds of vibe you're into—spicy? citrusy? boozy? licorice-y?—to better guide you toward something you'll love.

Tiny, Salty, Chocolatey Cookies

makes 24 cookies

6 tablespoons (¾ stick) unsalted butter

2½ cups confectioners' sugar

¾ cup unsweetened cocoa powder (see Note)

1 teaspoon kosher salt

2 large egg whites

1 large egg

8 ounces bittersweet chocolate (at least 67% cacao), chopped

½ cup finely chopped hazelnuts, almonds, pistachios, pecans, or walnuts (optional)

Flaky sea salt, such as Maldon or Jacobsen

NOTE *This is the time to invest in some high-quality unsweetened cocoa powder, since that's mostly what you'll be tasting here (that, and browned butter).*

I am not a chocolate person, but there are some occasions when I want a lightly sweet, definitely salty, chocolatey little something. In those moments, there is nothing better than this something, which I can best describe as the edges of a chewy brownie but in cookie form.

No special equipment, fancy techniques, or chilling time are needed, which means that even if you only bake cookies once a year, you can still make these. Perfect for the end of a meal, when you, too, have decided you've just *got* to have a chocolatey little something.

1 Preheat the oven to 350°F. Line two baking sheets with parchment.

2 Melt the butter in a small pot over medium heat, swirling, until starting to foam and brown, 3 to 4 minutes (whisk the butter from time to time so that the solids don't stick to the bottom of the pot). Let cool.

3 Whisk the confectioners' sugar, cocoa powder, and salt in a medium bowl, ridding it of as many lumps as possible (if you really want to, feel free to sift everything).

4 Using a spatula, mix in the egg whites, whole egg, and browned butter, stirring until you've got a good, smooth-ish mixture (any small lumps will take care of themselves), followed by the chocolate and any nuts you may want to add.

5 Using a spoon, drop quarter-sized blobs of dough (the texture is really somewhere between a dough and a batter), spacing about 2 inches apart on the baking sheet (they spread a lot). Sprinkle with flaky salt and bake until the cookies have flattened considerably and look baked through and a little wrinkled, 6 to 8 minutes. Let cool before eating so they can firm up.

DO AHEAD Cookies can be baked up to 2 days ahead, wrapped tightly, and stored at room temperature.

Lemony Turmeric Tea Cake

makes 1 loaf

1½ cups all-purpose flour

2 teaspoons baking powder

1 teaspoon kosher salt

¾ teaspoon ground turmeric

1 cup plus 2 tablespoons sugar

2 tablespoons finely grated lemon
zest, plus 2 tablespoons fresh
lemon juice (from about 1 lemon)

¾ cup sour cream or full-fat Greek
yogurt, plus more for serving
(optional)

2 large eggs

½ cup (1 stick) unsalted butter,
melted

½ lemon, thinly sliced, seeds
removed

Whipped cream (optional)

NOTE *For some reason,
finding a standard-size loaf
pan is nearly impossible, so get
as close to these dimensions
as you can. While you could
use either a metal or a glass
pan, I prefer metal because it
conducts heat more evenly.*

I don't want to oversell this cake, but I just want to say
that it's one of the more delicious things I've made in my
lifetime. I refer to it as "house cake," which is of course,
cake to keep in your house at all times. I am not what I
would call an earnest person, but in all earnestness just
slicing into it makes a bad day better, the baked equivalent
of burning sage or palo santo to clear the energy. It travels
well, and can truly be brought anywhere for any occasion,
but most of the time it never makes it out of my apartment.

1 Preheat the oven to 350°F. Lightly grease a 9 by 4-inch loaf
pan (see Note) with nonstick cooking spray or butter, and line
it with parchment, leaving some overhang on both of the longer
sides so you're able to easily lift the cake out after baking.

2 Whisk the flour, baking powder, salt, and turmeric in a
medium bowl.

3 In a large bowl, combine 1 cup of the sugar with the lemon zest
and rub together with your fingertips until the sugar is tinted
yellow and smells like you just rubbed a lemon in there. Whisk
in the sour cream, eggs, and the lemon juice until well blended.

4 Using a spatula, add the wet mixture to the flour mixture,
stirring just to blend. Fold in the melted butter. Scrape the
batter into the prepared pan, smoothing the top. Scatter the top
with the lemon slices and remaining 2 tablespoons sugar.

5 Bake until the top of the cake is golden brown, the edges
pull away from the sides of the pan, and a tester inserted in
the center comes out clean, 50 to 60 minutes. (I love deeply
caramelized lemon, but if they're getting too dark, lay a piece of
foil on top to prevent burning.) Let cool before slicing.

DO AHEAD Cake can be baked up to 5 days ahead, wrapped
tightly, and stored at room temperature.

Almost Angel Food Cake

serves 8 to 10

1½ cups cake (not self-rising)
   or all-purpose flour
¾ teaspoon baking powder
½ cup (1 stick) unsalted butter,
   melted and cooled
¼ cup canola oil
1 teaspoon vanilla extract
10 large egg whites
1½ cups sugar
½ teaspoon kosher salt
1 teaspoon fresh lemon juice

NOTE *If building this cake into another dessert is a step too many for you, you can simply bake this cake and serve it sliced with lots and lots of ice cream.*

This cake, while inspired by angel food cake, is not really angel food cake. But with its fluffy, egg-white batter, spongey, soakable texture, it almost is. Heavy on the vanilla and butter, the batter gets baked in a thin, even layer (as opposed to in a traditional thick angel food pan), giving you a golden brown, nearly crackling crust. Inside, it's porous and excellent for soaking—ideal for the faux tiramisu on page 296 or served with whipped cream and crushed berries.

1 Preheat the oven to 350°F. Line a standard 18 x 13-inch rimmed baking sheet with parchment paper.

2 In a large bowl, whisk the flour and baking powder together until no lumps remain. If you'd like, you can sift this mixture, knowing that this will be one of very few times I would even suggest such a thing; set aside.

3 In a small bowl, combine the butter, oil, and vanilla; set aside.

4 Using an electric mixer on medium-high, beat the egg whites till light, foamy, and frothy, a minute or two. Gradually add the sugar, a tablespoon or so at a time, letting the egg whites get more opaque and voluminous between additions, until sugar is incorporated. Add the salt and lemon juice and beat to blend.

5 Using a spatula, gently fold the flour mixture into the egg whites. Be gentle here, remembering that the goal is to keep this batter (and then the cake) as light, fluffy, and full of air as possible. Once the flour is nearly all the way incorporated, gently (!) fold in the butter mixture.

6 Spread out onto the prepared baking sheet, smoothing the top, and bake, rotating once, until golden brown and the cake is pulling away slightly from the sides of the pan, 18 to 20 minutes. Remove from the oven and let cool entirely.

DO AHEAD: Cake can be baked 2 days ahead, kept wrapped tightly at room temperature.

The Only Pie Crust

makes 2 discs of dough

2½ cups all-purpose flour

2 teaspoons sugar

1 teaspoon kosher salt

1¼ cups (2 sticks plus 4 tablespoons) unsalted butter, cut into 1-inch pieces, chilled

1 tablespoon apple cider vinegar or distilled white vinegar

¼ cup ice water, plus more as needed

NOTE *This recipe was published in my first book,* Dining In, *and since I really, truly believe it is The Only Pie Crust, here it is again.*

There is a lot to say about pie crusts in general, but know that the most important thing is: Too much water is the enemy of a good flaky crust. Most add more water than needed because they think the dough is too dry or hard to work with, but a dough that has just been mixed will never be easy to work with—that's why we rest it: to give it a chance to hydrate and relax; becoming easier to roll. So while it's occasionally necessary to add a tablespoon or two more of water to get the dough feeling good, don't go overboard!

1 Whisk the flour, sugar, and salt in a large bowl. Using your hands, smash the butter between your palms and fingertips into the flour, creating long, thin, flaky bits. When most of it is incorporated and there are no large chunks remaining, dump the flour mixture onto a work surface.

2 Combine the vinegar with the ice water and drizzle it over the flour. Using the tips of your fingers, run your hands through the flour mixture. Do this a few more times, until it all starts coming together.

3 Using the palms of your hand, start kneading the dough, gathering up any dry bits from the bottom and placing them on the top to be incorporated. You can add 1, maybe 2 tablespoons water during this process if you feel the dough really needs it, but it should remain on the drier side (it will hydrate and become more tender as it rests).

4 When you've got a shaggy mass of dough (it will not be smooth and it certainly will not be shiny), knead it one or two more times, then divide in half. Pat each half into a flat disc, about 1 inch thick. Wrap each disc individually and refrigerate at least 2 hours.

DO AHEAD This dough can be made up to 4 days ahead, tightly wrapped, and stored in the refrigerator; or made 1 month ahead, tightly wrapped in a resealable plastic bag, and frozen.

cleaning up nice

Cleaning up is a complicated and annoying thing that nobody wants to talk about. Doing dishes! That is not a sexy or cool topic, but we all have to do it, and if you're doing it right, it can be the most fun part of your evening. Take advantage of the fact that everyone is probably a little tipsy, put on some Janet Jackson, and start! washing! dishes! What was once a kitchen nightmare is now a full-blown dishwashing dance party, and the best part is that you don't have to do it alone. This is a technique I employ repeatedly and never feel the least bit guilty for it because everyone is having such a good time. (I swear! Right, guys? You like it, right?)

Of course, if at the end of the night, you'd all just really and truly rather not (I have been there—in fact, I am often there), waiting until the next morning to do dishes is fine. I just like to make sure that the table is at least cleared, the plates are at a minimum rinsed of food and stacked (because I am a Virgo and if I'm going to wake up to dirty dishes, at least they should be neatly stacked), and any edible food gets put away (because who doesn't love leftovers?).

acknowledgments

In a surprise to nobody, this is always the hardest thing to write because there were so many people involved and an abundance of wonderful people to thank. So in advance, if I forgot you, I am sorry! I owe you a glass of wine.

To my editor, Doris Cooper: If there is a word that means something greater than "patience," thank you for having it, specifically with me and this book. Thank you, also, for being my number one fan since day one and encouraging me to be nothing but myself. I adore our friendship and working relationship to the moon.

To my agent, Nicole Tourtelot: Thank you for always listening to me and shouldering my anxieties and standing up for me and believing in me even when (and especially when) I absolutely was not believing in me. "Be nicer to your book!" is now etched into my brain for all eternity. I am eternally grateful we found each other.

To everyone at Clarkson Potter who waited patiently for text and images and cover approvals and proofed art and words and messengered pages, specifically: Stephanie Huntwork, Kim Tyner, and Mark McCauslin; Kate Tyler, Windy Dorresteyn, Erica Gelbard, and Allison Renzulli in publicity and marketing; and, of course, Lydia O'Brien.

Aaron Wehner, who treats my books as if they were his very own. Thank you for your never-ending enthusiasm and support!

Michael Graydon and Nikole Herriott: Thank you for your insane hard work, patience, creativity, and flexibility. It is such a dream to collaborate with your brilliant minds. This book is as much yours as it is mine; I hope you feel that too. Thank you, also, for bringing Adam Katzowitz into our lives. Adam, you are a treasure trove of good vibes and positivity.

Kalen Kaminski: Thank you for lending your exquisite taste to the images, bringing your adventurous spirit to the long shoot days, and sourcing every small colored glass jar, plate, and dish within a 400-mile radius. And for bringing Erica Schwartzberg along for the ride. Erica, thank you for your hard work, enthusiasm, and hilarity; we adore you.

Elizabeth Spiridakis: My favorite work wife. Thank you for designing another beautiful, user-friendly, easy-to-navigate, thoughtful layout for this book. Thank you for letting me invade your personal life and working till the wee hours of the morning on this baby. I adore you endlessly.

Lauren Schaeffer and Susan Kim: I honestly don't have enough space to declare the depths of my appreciation and love for you both. You're my positive angels on set, off set, on text, on email, in cars, at the grocery store, at markets, at butcher shops. Thank you for everything you do to keep the food looking beautiful, the recipes working, and everybody's (my) stress levels at a minimum. You're my whole heart!

Yewande Komolafe and Luciana Lamboy: Thank you for your thorough testing notes to make sure these recipes work, without which this book would be totally useless.

To my New York Times Cooking and Bon Appétit family, especially Emily Weinstein, Sam Sifton, Krysten Chambrot, Adam Rapoport, Julia Kramer, Meryl Rothstein, Amiel Stanek, and Christina Chaey: Thank you for giving my recipes and words a home in your newspaper and magazine and for editing me to greatness. I feel so lucky to work with each and every one of you. I'm sorry for blowing past all my deadlines, but now that this book is finished, I'll be on time forever (mostly!).

Molly Mandel, thank you SO much for your guidance, encouragement, honesty, and sense of humor about all the things. I adore you and can't wait to keep working together.

Julia Schniederman and Eli Joyce: Thank you for your assisting, reading, errand running, cleaning, and schedule keeping, without which, I would be totally useless.

To my friends and family who are always down to come over for dinner, bring wine, and then clean up, all while being photographed: Michael, Eva, Mercedez, Ben, Julia, Yos, Hannah, Anoop, Elliott, Stan, James, Glo, Dana, Blake, and John.

Kate, Lilli, and Julia: Thank you for the FaceTimes and the incessant texts and for keeping me grounded, sane, and functioning. I love you so much.

Greta Lee and Russ Armstrong: Thank you for always letting me invade your home and pretending I live there. I love you both almost as much as I love garlic scapes. To Hannah and JD, thank you for letting us stay in your Livingston Manor manor, truly a dreamy space to create in.

To everyone who lent me a home to be alone and write: Sarah and Sohail Zandi from Brushland Eating House (thank you, Bovina!); Emily, Joey, and the whole Fleishaker family (thank you, Santa Fe!); and Sarina Dailey and Chris Parachini (thank you, Rockaway Beach!).

To my mom, dad, stepmom, sister, brother, aunt, uncle, and grandmother: You are my favorite people to receive texts of my recipes from. Thank you for cooking and loving me so much.

To every small business, independent bookstore, and major retailer who supported Dining In, stocked it on your shelves, and recommended it to customers: I am forever grateful.

To everyone who bought Dining In, cooked The Stew, baked The Cookies, subscribed to New York Times Cooking or read Bon Appétit: Thank you, thank you, thank you. I am overwhelmed with gratitude that you're cooking (and presumably liking!) the recipes I put into the world, which is the only reason I do it. Thank you for your support and enthusiasm, which allows me to continue doing this dream job.

index